Macedonian Warrior

Alexander's elite infantryman

Waldemar Heckel & Ryan Jones • Illustrated by Christa Hook

First published in Great Britain in 2006 by Osprey Publishing, Midland House, West Way, Botley, Oxford OX2 0PH, UK
443 Park Avenue South, New York, NY 10016, USA
E-mail: info@ospreypublishing.com

A CIP catalog record for this book is available from the British Library

ISBN 1 84176 950 9

Page layout by Ken Vail Graphic Design, Cambridge (kvgd.com)
Index by Alan Thatcher
Originated by United Grahics, Singapore
Printed in China through World Print Ltd.

06 07 08 09 10   10 9 8 7 6 5 4 3 2 1

FOR A CATALOG OF ALL BOOKS PUBLISHED BY OSPREY MILITARY AND AVIATION PLEASE CONTACT:

NORTH AMERICA
Osprey Direct, c/o Random House Distribution Center, 400 Hahn Road, Westminster, MD 21157
E-mail: info@ospreydirect.com

ALL OTHER REGIONS
Osprey Direct UK, P.O. Box 140 Wellingborough, Northants, NN8 2FA, UK
E-mail: info@ospreydirect.co.uk

www.ospreypublishing.com

Artist's note

Readers may care to note that the original paintings from which the color plates in this book were prepared are available for private sale. All reproduction copyright whatsoever is retained by the Publishers. All inquiries should be addressed to:

Scorpio Gallery
PO Box 475, Hailsham, East Sussex BN27 2SL, UK

The Publishers regret that they can enter into no correspondence upon this matter.

Editor's note

Every attempt has been made by the publisher to secure the appropriate permissions for materials reproduced in this book. If there has been any oversight we will be happy to rectify the situation and written submission should be made to the publishers.

CONTENTS

MACEDONIAN WARRIOR: ALEXANDER'S ELITE INFANTRYMAN

INTRODUCTION

Greek land warfare before the age of Alexander the Great was primarily, and often exclusively, infantry warfare. Chariots had been used in the Bronze Age – either as moving and elevated platforms for archers or as vehicles that simply delivered prominent warriors to the battlefield – but in the Near East and Anatolia the effectiveness of the chariot was negated by new tactics and weaponry, and in the Greek peninsula it had always been of limited value because of the nature of the terrain. The difficulties of topography created similar problems for the unshod horse. Although some regions like Thessaly and Boeotia were more conducive to cavalry warfare, the numbers of mounted troops were limited by the expense of maintaining horses, and few 'horsemen' were actually trained to fight in cavalry formation. So it was that nature and economics made the Greeks infantrymen – 'men of the spear.'

By the mid-seventh century BC, the Greeks had begun to develop the weaponry and style of close-ordered combat that we call 'hoplite warfare,' in which soldiers fought in ranks, usually eight men deep, although the depth varied according to the numbers a state could muster for battle and the length of the line (i.e. the 'frontage'). The hoplite (plural: *hoplitai*) was thus a heavily armed infantryman, named perhaps for the large shield he carried (the *hoplon*, although *hopla* in the plural means 'arms' in general). He was also protected by a helmet – of which the most common was the Corinthian type – that gave protection to the head and most of the face, a bronze cuirass, and often greaves. The weapon of choice for the Greeks was the spear (*dory*), about 7–8ft in length, including spearhead and butt spike. The sword, by comparison, was the weapon of last resort and, indeed, incompatible with the dense formation and the pushing techniques (*othismos*) of the phalanx. Although minor changes occurred in the shape and construction of the cuirass or the style of the helmet, the appearance and operations of hoplite armies did not change dramatically over the centuries, nor did the Greeks, despite their overall reputation for inventiveness, show much

Head of Alexander the Great. (Topfoto.co.uk, Art Media-Pella Museum)

interest in deviating from a tried and true method of warfare. It is, in fact, an indication of the nature of early Greek warfare, which sought to settle issues quickly and decisively (in a single engagement, if possible), that heavy infantry battle was preferred in a land better suited to other types of troops. It was only when the goals of war and the attempts to extend power significantly – as in the case of the Peloponnesian War (431–404 BC) – brought the Greeks to a state of what approximated 'total war,' that lasting changes (as opposed to experiments) in the manner of waging war began to be made. Perhaps the most significant of these changes was the creation of the Macedonian phalanx and the *sarissa*-bearing infantrymen, who are the subject of this volume.

Gold medallion from Tarsus showing the head of Philip II, the architect of the Macedonian phalanx. (Topfoto.co.uk, Ann Ronan Picture Library)

Historical background

The great struggles with Persia in the early fifth century BC had not only proved the worth of the Spartan army, but also molded Athens into a new military power both on land and at sea. Historians call the period from 478 to 431 BC, between the Greek victory over the forces of Xerxes and the beginning of the Peloponnesian War, the 'Fifty Years' (*Pentekontaetia*). This period witnessed the growth of the Delian League, a defensive alliance against Persia under Athenian leadership, and its transformation into the Athenian Empire. The interests of this new empire regularly collided with those of the Peloponnesian League, of which Sparta was the hegemon – in short, the director of its foreign policy and commander of its armies. It was natural, if not inevitable, that the two powers and their allies should come into conflict. So great were the resources of each side, and the respective implications of victory and defeat, that the Athenian statesman, Thucydides, decided to record the events of this struggle from the very beginning, thinking that it would be 'a great war, and more worthy of relation than any that preceded it' (Thucydides, 1.1). In this he was not disappointed, although he either did not live long enough to finish his work or abandoned the project before completion. The Peloponnesian War, as it came to be known, culminated in the utter defeat of the Athenians, and it was not long before many would regret the destruction of the balance of power, which had given a fragile stability to the Greek world.

For Sparta, victory was a mixed blessing. The exercise of its new supremacy proved financially ruinous, and destroyed both the social underpinnings of Sparta's military forces and its reputation for invincibility. Furthermore, it was regarded as arbitrary and unfair by Sparta's former allies who, instead of sharing the spoils of victory, found that they had merely contributed to their own subordination. Spartan navarchs (fleet commanders) ruled the Aegean and garrisons commanded by its harmosts (city governors or prefects) supported unpopular decarchies in cities that had rebelled from Athens in the

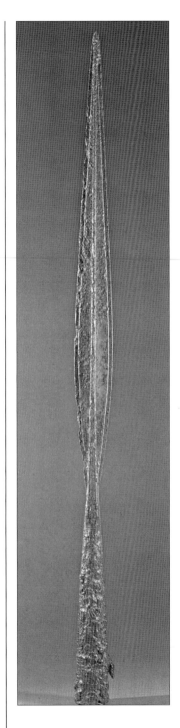

The *sarissa* head found at Vergina and first published by the Greek archaeologist, M. Andronikos. It measures $20\frac{1}{8}$in (51cm) in length and weighs 2.7lb (1.235kg). (From the Vergina excavation site. Archaeological Museum, Thessaloniki)

hope of gaining liberation. The most prominent of the disaffected states, Thebes and Corinth, soon formed an alliance with Athens and Argos, the age-old enemies of Sparta, and challenged the new leader of Greece in the Corinthian War (from 394 to 387/6). But Sparta, as it had done in the late stages of the Peloponnesian War, relied upon the support of Persia and the promise of gold from the Persian Great King to impose upon the Greek world a 'common peace,' which guaranteed local autonomy but in fact maintained Spartan supremacy. This peace, known as the 'King's Peace' or 'Peace of Antalcidas,' failed to respect the integrity of the Boeotian League, which was politically dominated by Thebes, and bitterness between Sparta and its former ally continued through the 380s and 370s until the Thebans, having adopted new infantry tactics, dealt the Spartans a crippling blow at the battle of Leuctra (371).

It was during the brief period of Theban military supremacy in the 360s that the upstart state intervened in the affairs of Thessaly and Macedonia, and as a consequence of these political events Philip, the youngest of the three sons of the Macedonian king Amyntas III and now in his early teens, was held as a hostage in Thebes. The military society of Thebes, the fame of the Sacred Band (see page 52), and the inspirational Theban general Epaminondas all had an impact on the impressionable and intelligent youth. When Philip assumed the kingship of Macedon after the military disaster against the Illyrians in 360/59, which took the life of King Perdiccas III (son of Amyntas III) and a large number of Macedonian *hetairoi* (the most prestigious of the mounted troops and king's companions), he found himself in a precarious position from which he would have to extricate himself by a combination of diplomacy and military innovation. Diplomacy would be the hallmark of Philip's reign – and indeed it was said that he took greater pride in the victories won without battle – but his military innovations also had an impact that was both immediate and enduring.

> Philip was not panic-stricken by the magnitude of the expected perils, but, bringing together the Macedonians in a series of assemblies and exhorting them with eloquent speeches to be men, he built up their morale, and, having improved the organization of his forces and equipped the men suitably with weapons of war, he held constant maneuvers of the men under arms and competitive drills. Indeed he devised the compact order and the equipment of the phalanx imitating the close order fighting with overlapping shields of the warriors at Troy and was the first to organize the Macedonian phalanx. (Diodorus of Sicily, 16.3.1–2)

Writing in the eight or seventh century BC, Homer in the *Iliad* refers to this phalanx when he talks about Greek troops fitting together 'helmet and studded shields, pressing shield upon shield, helmet upon helmet and man upon man' (16.214–15), and in Book 13 of the same work:

> There stood the very pick of their best men … an impenetrable hedge of spears and sloping shields, shield-to-shield, helmet-to-helmet, man-to-man. So close were the ranks that, when they

The shield monument on the plain of Leuctra, where the Thebans in 371 destroyed the supremacy of the Spartan army and established for themselves a brief period of hegemony. (Author's collection)

moved their heads, their crested helmets with their shining plates touched and the spears overlapped as they brandished them in their sturdy hands.

The description is echoed by Quintus Curtius Rufus in his *History of Alexander*, written in the first century AD:

> The Macedonian line is certainly coarse and inelegant, but it protects behind its shields and lances immovable wedges of tough, densely packed soldiers. The Macedonians call it a phalanx, an infantry column that holds its ground. They stand man next to man, arms interlocked with arms. They wait eagerly for their commander's signal, and they are trained to follow the standards and not break ranks. (3.2.13)

These passages nevertheless tell us little about the weaponry and organization of Philip's infantry, and in most cases we can do little more than consider what the Alexander historians tell us and work back from these sources. In this study of the Macedonian infantry an attempt has been made to distinguish between the theoretical constructs of the mid-to-late Hellenistic period (i.e. the works of Asclepiodotus and later tacticians) and the Alexander sources, which, although late, are based on contemporary writings. Some later evidence can be used to present aspects of infantry equipment and warfare that can be regarded as typical, but for the specific details of life and practice in the later fourth century, the works of the Alexander historians, supplemented by artistic representations and archaeological finds, will have to suffice. To go beyond that – without indicating where the evidence ends and speculation begins – would be misleading.

CHRONOLOGY

*c.*650 BC Early hoplite armies. Hoplites are associated with the rise of the middle class and establishment of tyrannies in the Greek world.

490 Battle of Marathon. The Athenians and a band of Plataeans defeat Darius I's general, Datis, and repel the first Persian invasion of Greece.

480–79 Xerxes, son of Darius I, invades Greece. Battles of Thermopylae and Artemisium; Salamis. After Salamis, Xerxes returns to Asia and the Greeks defeat his lieutenant, Mardonius, at Plataea (479).

478–31 The 'Fifty Years:' the defensive alliance against Persia known as the Delian League is transformed into an Athenian Empire.

431–04 The Peloponnesian War. Fought between the Athenians, with their empire and allies, and the Spartan-led Peloponnesian League.

394–87/6 The Corinthian War. Sparta survives a challenge by a coalition of Athens, Argos, Corinth, and Thebes.

387/6 The Peace of Antalcidas ('King's Peace'). The peace guarantees 'local autonomy' but in fact it amounts to little more than 'divide and conquer.'

*c.*378 Innovations of Iphicrates. The Athenian mercenary commander arms his infantrymen with the lighter shield (*pelte*) and a spear measuring about 12ft in length.

371 Battle of Leuctra. The Thebans defeat the Spartan army under King Cleombrotus. The victory marks the end of Spartan military supremacy.

368–65 Philip son of Amyntas, the future king of Macedon, resides in Thebes as a hostage.

362 Battle of Mantinea. An indecisive battle in which the brilliant general Epaminondas is killed; this signals the rapid decline of Theban power.

360/59 Death of Macedonian king Perdiccas III in battle with the Illyrians. Some 4,000 Macedonians are killed in the engagement. Accession of Philip II.

359/8 Philip II fights the Illyrians, using a reformed army, and forces them to cede the territory east of Lake Lychnitis.

338 Philip II victorious over Athenians and Thebans at Chaeronea. Alexander fights on the Macedonian left, where his forces destroy the Sacred Band.

337 Formation of the League of Corinth. Philip II is elected as its military leader (*hegemon*).

336 Philip II murdered as he enters the theatre at Aegae (Vergina); accession of Alexander III ('The Great').

336–35 Alexander's campaigns in the north against the Thracians, Triballians, and Illyrians. He then moves south and destroys Thebes, killing its men and selling the women and children into slavery.

334 Alexander crosses to Asia Minor. He defeats a coalition of satraps (governors of provinces) at the Granicus River. Some cities, like Sardis, surrender to him, but Miletus and Halicarnassus are defended by troops of the Persian king and must be taken by siege.

333 Alexander undoes (i.e. 'cuts') the Gordian Knot, which promises him mastery of Asia. He defeats Darius III at the battle of Issus.

332 Sieges of Tyre (seven months) and Gaza (two months).

332/1 Alexander in Egypt. He consults the Oracle of Amun at Siwah in the Libyan desert (just west of the Qattara Depression), where he is proclaimed 'Son of Amun.' He founds Alexandria on the Nile Delta.

331 Battle of Gaugamela (Arbela). Alexander defeats Darius a second time in the largest and bloodiest

Ivory head of Philip from the so-called Tomb of Philip II in Vergina. The right eye appears to have suffered damage. We know that Philip lost his right eye to an arrow at Methone in 353 BC, and that a wonderful feat of surgery by the doctor, Critobulus, saved him from serious disfigurement. (Archaeological Museum, Thessaloniki)

battle to date. This is followed by the surrender of the Persian capitals, Babylon and Susa, and by Macedonian military reforms.

330   Alexander captures Persepolis and burns its palace. In May he crosses the Zagros mountains and secures Ecbatana. Darius III is arrested and killed by his own men; Alexander comes upon Darius' corpse beyond the Caspian Gates and gives it a royal burial.

329–27   Campaigns in Bactria (modern Afghanistan) and Sogdiana. A long guerrilla war is ended when Alexander marries Rhoxane, the daughter of a native warlord named Oxyartes.

327   Alexander moves against India and campaigns in the Swat region.

326   Battle of the Hydaspes. Alexander defeats the Indian rajah Porus. The troops mutiny at the Hyphasis (or Beas) River. Formation of the argyraspids ('silver shields.')

325   Return from India. The bulk of the heavy infantry and the *apomachoi* return via the Bolan Pass; Alexander leads the other troops through the Gedrosian desert, where they endure great hardships.

324   Military reforms. Alexander integrates barbarians into his army.

323   Death of Alexander. Dispute over the succession.

318   The argyraspids join the commander and governor Eumenes, who challenges the authority of Antigonus the One-Eyed (also a Macedonian commander and governor).

317/6   Battles of Paraetacene and Gabiene. The argyraspids surrender Eumenes to Antigonus, who has him killed. But the argyraspids, too, are dispersed and consigned to hard campaigning in the East.

301   The battle of Ipsus. The infantry of Antigonus the One-Eyed, unsupported by the cavalry of the impetuous young Demetrius, is defeated by the forces of Lysimachus and Seleucus.

FROM HERDSMAN TO INFANTRYMAN

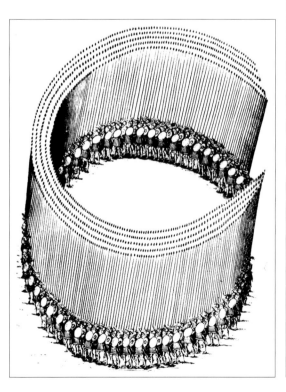

A 16th-century engraving of a Macedonian phalanx carrying the long *sarissa* lances. (Bibliothèque Nationale, Paris)

What was it that distinguished the Macedonian infantryman from the Greek hoplite? The answer seems at first obvious – the Macedonians fought with smaller shields and longer spears (*sarissai*) – but upon closer inspection proves to be less so. The problem is made no easier by the fact that Macedonian infantrymen, both the *sarissa*-bearing phalangites and the hypaspists, are on occasions referred to, loosely, as 'hoplites.' However, the principles behind the Macedonian infantry reforms and the reasons for the success of the phalanx are clear enough. Unlike many of the Greek states south of Mt Olympus and the Peneus River, Macedon did not lack manpower. Rather it lacked major urban centers and a solid middle class from which to draw hoplites who could afford their own military equipment. On the other hand, the Macedonian soldier was not the typical Greek farmer, who tilled the land to which he was tied both by the labor-intensive nature of farming and by the agricultural calendar. Many Macedonians were herdsmen who tended and followed their herds according to the offerings of the seasons, and whose duties could be handled in many cases by the old or the young, or the women. From such peasant stock, hardy and accustomed to the simple life, the

Macedonian kings could draw full-time 'professional' soldiers, who were no doubt attracted by the prospect of supplementing their meager incomes by plunder.

In his speech to the Macedonians at Opis on the Tigris River in 324, Alexander reminds his troops:

> Philip took you over when you were helpless vagabonds, mostly clothed in skins, feeding a few animals on the mountains and engaged in their defence in unsuccessful fighting with Illyrians, Triballians and the neighbouring Thracians. He gave you cloaks to wear instead of skins, he brought you down from the mountains to the plains; he made you a match in battle for the barbarians on your borders, so that you no longer trusted for your safety to the strength of your positions so much as to your natural courage. (Arrian, 7.9.2)

In a short time, the Macedonian herdsmen had exchanged the 'fruitless labors on the sheer rocks and crags of Illyria and Thrace' for 'the spoils of the entire East' (Curtius Rufus, 3.10.6). But it remains to explain their success. Obviously, if Philip could not put a native hoplite army of any size into the field after his brother King Perdiccas III's Illyrian disaster, where 4,000 Macedonians including the king himself were slain, he would have to rely on mercenaries – whom, in Macedon's current political and economic state, he could ill afford – or he would have to provide his men with a distinct advantage, either in weaponry or tactics (if not both), over their enemies. Compact formations alone will not explain his success, and Philip will scarcely have had time to train his demoralized men in new tactics, except of course to apply what he had learned in Thebes about attacking a point in the enemy line in depth. Furthermore, to attribute Philip's overnight success to the adoption of Theban tactics disparages the difficulty of the action. The only plausible explanation is that Philip experimented, right from the start, with a new weapon.

Longer spears were certainly not a Macedonian invention. They are attested in the art of the Bronze Age and on Near Eastern reliefs. An extended spear was introduced in the early 370s by the Athenian mercenary commander Iphicrates who, we are told, equipped his men with lighter shields and spears that were half again as long as the regular hoplite spear (that is, about 12ft in length). Massed, densely packed formations armed with a longer spear could keep more heavily armored and better trained hoplites out of range, and could use the weight of their formation to break the traditional hoplite line.

ENLISTMENT

What evidence we have indicates that the Macedonian kings recruited their infantrymen in two ways. The bulk of the heavy infantry, who during Alexander's campaigns appear to have been known as *pezhetairoi*, or 'foot companions,' and who numbered about 9,000, were clearly regional levies, commanded by members of their own aristocracies. Hence we are told of one unit (*taxis*) comprising the Orestians and Lyncestians and of another composed of Tymphaeans, just as we hear of cavalry squadrons (*ilai*) recruited from cities like Amphipolis, Anthemus, and Apollonia. As far as the Macedonian peasantry and their 'tribal' rulers were concerned, this organization reflected the age-old pattern of life in the mountain cantons that had only recently been merged into the greater Macedonian state. They were proud of their origins and loyal to their commanders, and thus the training school for future officers, the *paides basilikoi* or 'royal pages,' was located at the court of Pella where the sons of the Upper Macedonian nobles served as useful hostages and were taught to place the needs of the state above those of the region.

Not only were the commanders (*taxiarchai*) also from the same regions as their troops, but an individual *taxis* was sometimes commanded by members of the same family on different occasions. Thus we find the Tymphaeans commanded at the Granicus River by Amyntas son of Andromenes, at Issus by his brother Simmias, and in India by another brother, Attalus. That Alexander's six *taxeis* of *pezhetairoi* were divided between Upper and Lower Macedonians is also unproved, and indeed unlikely. The names of all the known *taxiarchai* in the first three years of the campaign suggest Upper Macedonian origins – there is certainly no definitely attested Lower Macedonian phalanx commander – and it would be extremely unlikely that half or two-thirds of the *pezhetairoi* were led by officers of their own region, whereas the remainder were not. At least half the total number of infantry remained in Macedonia with the regent, Antipater, and it would make good sense to assume that those from the politically volatile areas, like the cantons of Upper Macedonia, would be removed from the homeland and kept under Alexander's watchful eye.

By contrast, the hypaspists were an elite force, chosen on an individual basis for their physical strength and valor. For this reason, a portion of them constituted the Guard (the *agema*) and all 3,000 of them were stationed between the *pezhetairoi* and the cavalry, where the king himself directed affairs. Recruitment was based on social standing, and the hypaspists were divided into 'regular' and 'royal' hypaspists (*hypaspistai basilikoi*). Those who commanded the regular hypaspists, as chiliarchs or pentakosiarchs, were selected on the basis of valor, although their overall commander, the *archihypaspistes*, was a Macedonian noble appointed by the king.

TRAINING

The Alexander historians say very little about training, but Diodorus, commenting on Philip's reforms, emphasizes training and discipline alongside the introduction of new equipment (16.3.1–2). Polyaenus

Wallpainting from the tomb of Lyson and Callicles in Lefkadia, depicting a corselet on an armor stand, topped by a helmet with cheek pieces. A *xiphos* can be seen to the right. (Ekdotike Athenon SA, Athens)

(*Stratagemata* 4.2.10) relates that Philip trained his men by forcing them to march 300 stades (over 30 miles) in a single day, wearing their helmets and greaves, and carrying their shields, *sarissai*, and their daily provisions. Indeed, Philip sought to improve the mobility and efficiency of the army by limiting the infantry to one servant for every ten men – or, presumably, per *dekas*, which could number as many as 16 men – and ordering the troops to carry rations of grain sufficient for 30 days (Frontinus, *Strat.* 4.1.6). In this respect they anticipated Marius' famous 'mules' (*muli Mariani*) of the late Roman Republic. Other luxuries were frowned upon: we are told of a Tarentine officer (though presumably a cavalryman) who was stripped of his command for taking warm baths; 'for he did not understand the ways of the Macedonians, among whom not even a woman who has just given birth bathes in warm water' (Polyaenus, *Strat.* 4.2.1).

Actual tactical maneuvers were also practiced, for neither Philip's orderly feigned 'retreat' at Chaeronea nor Alexander's dazzling display before the Illyrians at Pellium could have been executed without regular training. Indeed, we are told that Alexander, upon his accession, gave particular attention to 'the use of weapons and tactical exercises' (Diodorus, 17.2.3), but further details are lacking. The *sarissa* was awkward to handle at the best of times, and the entanglement of these weapons could spell disaster. Hence even in open formation, movement in unison was a practiced art, though admittedly when the pushing started it was courage and strength that prevailed over style.

In his campaign against the Illyrian chieftains Glaucias and Cleitus Alexander had occasion to use a variation of parade-ground drill to intimidate the enemy, and from the description that follows, we can see just what sorts of moves were rehearsed:

Alexander drew up the main body of his infantry in mass formation 120 deep, posting on either wing 200 cavalrymen with instructions to make no noise, and to obey orders smartly. Then he gave the order for the heavy infantry first to erect their spears, and afterwards, at the word of command, to lower the massed points as if for attack, swinging them, again at the word of command, now to the right, now to the left. The whole phalanx he then moved smartly forward, and, wheeling it this way and that, caused it to execute various intricate movements. Having thus put his troops with great rapidity through a number of different formations, he ordered his left to form a wedge and advanced to the attack. (Arrian, 1.6.1–3)

In this case the initial leveling of the *sarissa* was for visual effect, to overawe the enemy, and it scarcely needs to be said that the purpose of drill is as much to intimidate the enemy as to gain proficiency in battle.

Macedonian royal symbol, the eight-rayed star, on three golden disks found in Tomb II at Vergina. (From the Vergina excavation site. Archaeological Museum, Thessaloniki)

The simple display of the Macedonian army in formation was sufficient in 336/5 to dissuade the Thebans from rebelling, for the sight of the phalanx brought back vivid memories of the disaster at Chaeronea. The historian Diodorus, perhaps repeating the words of a contemporary source, describes Alexander's army as arrayed *kataplêktikôs* ('in a way that caused fear or consternation', 17.4.4). But intimidating drill could also be used for practical effect, as when in the campaign north of the Danube the leveled *sarissai* acted as scythes to destroy the crops in the field, an action which served also to ferret out any of the enemy who might have taken shelter there.

APPEARANCE AND EQUIPMENT

Sarissa

The trademark of the Macedonian phalanx was the *sarissa*, a pike of cornel wood measuring as much as 12 cubits (18ft) in Alexander's time, according to the only contemporary source for such information, Theophrastus (*Hist. Pl.* 3.12.2). By 300 BC, the length had increased in some cases to 16 cubits (24 ft) (Polyaenus, *Stratagemata* 2.29.2), but it is important to remember that we are dealing with maximum lengths, and many *sarissai* may have been shorter. Asclepiodotus (*Tact.* 5.1), a tactical writer of the first century BC, comments that the shortest Macedonian pike was 10 cubits (15ft), and we may assume that, in the time of Philip II and Alexander, *sarissai* measured 15–18ft. *Sarissa* heads found at Chaeronea are in a poor state of preservation, but one found near the tombs of Vergina has a socket that measures $1\frac{7}{16}$ in in diameter, and, even if we allow for tapering, it is probably safe to assume that shaft of the *sarissa* was between $1\frac{1}{4}$ and $1\frac{1}{2}$ inches in diameter. The *sarissa* head from Vergina measures $20\frac{1}{8}$ in in length and weighs $2\frac{1}{2}$ lb. Butt spikes were somewhat shorter and lighter, $17\frac{1}{2}$ in in length and weighing 2.4lb. The weight of the entire *sarissa* measuring 18ft and including a coupling

Painting from the tomb of Lyson and Callicles in Lefkadia. The center depicts a shield with the eight-rayed star of Macedonia. Below it are greaves and helmets; the one on the left is of the Thracian type, and the sword on the upper left, which has a hilt in the style of a bird's head, appears to be a *kopis*. The sword on the right is the straight, double-edged *xiphos*. (Ekdotike Athenon SA, Athens)

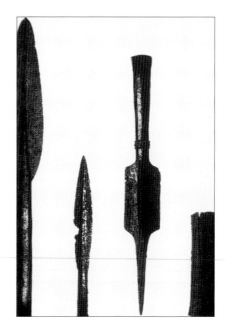

TOP LEFT **The *sarissa* head, spearhead, *sarissa* butt spike and coupling link (or collar) from Vergina, taken from the official publication in *Bulletin de Correspondence Hellenique* by M. Andronikos. (From the Vergina excavation site. Archaeological Museum, Thessaloniki)**

TOP RIGHT **Detail of the *sarissa* butt spike and coupling link (or collar). The butt spike is 17in in length and weighs 2lb 7oz; the coupling link is $6\frac{1}{8}$ in long. (Archaeological Museum, Thessaloniki)**

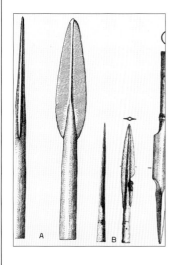

ABOVE **Drawings of the *sarissa* head, spearhead, and *sarissa* butt spike from Vergina, taken from the official publication in *Bulletin de Correspondence Hellenique* by M. Andronikos. Cf. the photo of these items plus the coupling link or collar at the top of the page. (Archaeological Museum, Thessaloniki)**

device was probably 14–15lb, about seven times the weight of an average hoplite spear.

An essential feature of the *sarissa* was the coupling device, the one surviving example measuring $6\frac{3}{8}$in, which gave the weapon added sturdiness, improved balance and decreased the bend – even though cornel wood is surprisingly sturdy. It also allowed the weapon to be dismantled and carried in two parts on the march, and it must have facilitated repair or replacement of weapon parts. The butt spike acted not only as a counterweight, but could be used as a weapon-point if the front of the *sarissa* was broken. (That the phalangite or the hypaspist carried a javelin in addition to the *sarissa* is doubtful: see the discussion of Plate E on page 61.)

Shield

Because the *sarissa* was wielded with both hands, the size and shape of the shield was also changed. Instead of the concave, larger shield of the hoplite (the radius of which was roughly a cubit ($1\frac{1}{2}$ft), since the arm was drawn through a central arm band (*porpax*) up to the inside of the elbow and the hand gripped a leather thong attached to the rim), the Macedonian phalangite now carried a smaller, less concave shield, which was eight palms in diameter (about 2ft) and lacking a rim. The shield (*pelte*) had an elbow sling and was suspended over the shoulder by a baldric, but since we have only found remains of metal coverings, there is no certainty about the existence of a grip (*antilabe*). Something of this sort – perhaps made of leather – must have existed, however, or the *pezhetairos* who had either broken or lost his *sarissa* would have found the shield all but useless. The bronze covering of such a shield has survived at Begora in Lyncus (Upper Macedonia) and, despite the loss of the wooden center and some damage to the covering itself, it corresponds closely to the description of the Macedonian shield given by Asclepiodotus (*Tact.* 5.1). Furthermore, the shield has the eight-rayed star of Macedonia embossed on it and bears an inscription that might be

14

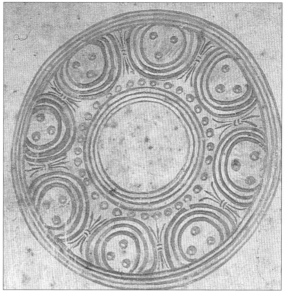

LEFT **Wallpainting from Boscoreale, Villa of Fannius Synistor, based on a mid-third century BC original. It shows what is thought by some to be Antigonus Gonatas (grandson of Antigonus the One-Eyed) wearing the *kausia*. Beside him is a Macedonian shield, decorated with the eight-rayed star. This is apparently a ceremonial shield rather than a functional one. The woman may be his mother, Phila, but others have argued that the scene shows Alexander IV and Rhoxane. (Ekdotike Athenon SA, Athens)**

ABOVE **Wallpainting from the tomb of Lyson and Callicles (*c*.250 BC) at Lefkadia depicting a shield that resembles in decoration that on the Boscoreale Mural of Antigonus Gonatas. (Ekdotike Athenon SA, Athens)**

reconstructed as 'of King Antigonus.' In Egypt a mold for a similar shield with the inscription 'of King Ptolemy' shows that these were mass produced and, as in the case of the butt spike mentioned below, represented government issue.

Armor

The remainder of the infantryman's equipment can be discerned from Polyaenus' account of Macedonian training, where it is said that the soldier marched with his helmet (*kranos*), shield (*pelte*, not *hoplon* or *aspis*), greaves (*knemides*), and his pike (*sarissa*). There is, significantly, no mention of the cuirass or corselet. This is echoed in the regulations for soldiers from Amphipolis (albeit from the time of Philip V, who reigned from 221 to 179 BC), which also make no mention of the cuirass (see Austin no. 74, quoted on page 24) except for officers. Infantrymen must therefore either have dispensed with the bronze or leather cuirass or have worn the lighter *linothorax* (a cuirass made of glued layers of linen). The wearing of some kind of breastplate, at least in the front ranks, appears to be confirmed by Polyaenus (*Stratagemata* 4.3.13), who claims that Alexander armed those who had previously fled in battle with the *hemithorakion* ('half-thorax,' which covered only the front of the body), instead of the regular thorax, in order that they would not turn their backs to the enemy. But corselets of any kind may have been unnecessary for those fighting closer to the back of the phalanx, and there must have been many occasions when Macedonian kings,

constrained by lack of equipment or lack of funds, put men into the field with inferior armor. Complete uniformity in weaponry and appearance is – with the notable exception of the Late Roman infantryman – a rather modern phenomenon.

Greaves, which had been used less frequently by Greek hoplites (Hanson, *Hoplites*, 76; Snodgrass, *Arms and Armor*, 110), appear to be a standard feature, and the Amphipolis regulations prescribe a fine for those who did not maintain and wear them. The explanation for their necessity may be as simple as the fact that the butt spikes of the *sarissai* could easily harm the legs of soldiers in the formation.

Helmets were of the conical or Phrygian type, with or without cheek guards and nothing to protect the bridge of the nose. But the advantages clearly outweighed the lack of protection, since the troops had greater hearing and visibility, to say nothing of the stifling heat that must have built up inside the Corinthian-style helmet. At any rate, in Classical Greek armies of the late fifth and early fourth centuries BC, many hoplites had already moved to the less constricting *pilos* helmet, and others adopted the Chalcidian style, which gave some protection to the bridge of the nose. It is reasonable to suppose that all types were represented in the Macedonian phalanx, and that fully functional equipment was often stripped from the dead and used by the victors. Helmets must, however, have been used only by the men in the first few ranks, those in the back rows wearing the *kausia*, which resembled a beret.

Sword or blade

Finally, the historians do not mention a secondary weapon for the phalangites, though clearly they must have had them. Polyaenus' omission

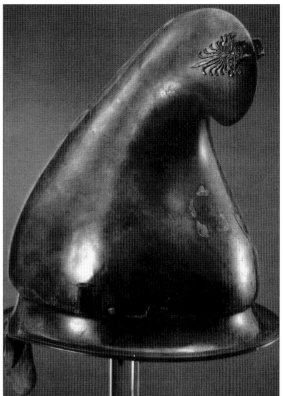

may be an oversight, since the *machaira* blade is listed as a standard piece of equipment in the Amphipolis regulations of Philip V. Nevertheless, the terminology is not clear. The *xiphos* was apparently the shorter, double-edged sword, whereas the slashing weapon, the *kopis* (or 'cleaver'), was longer, curved, and more suitable for cavalrymen. By contrast the *machaira* could be a shorter, curved knife – and it is often translated as a 'dagger' – used for dispatching the defeated foe. Yet, Xenophon uses *machaira* as the equivalent of *kopis*. Hence if the Macedonian phalangite carried the *kopis*, it was for use in open fighting, where the formation had disintegrated, and possibly a later addition to his equipment, resulting from the experience of fighting the Romans, whose weapon of choice was the sword (see Anderson, *Hoplite Weapons*, 26–7).

Uniformity of appearance

There remains the question of whether the *pezhetairoi* and the hypaspists were armed in the same fashion. Some influential modern historians, such as W. W. Tarn, G. T. Griffith, and R. D. Milns, have argued that there was no significant difference in armament, but military writers are coming around to the opposite view. The Alexander Sarcophagus shows a Macedonian fighter, in the midst of the cavalry fray, carrying a slightly smaller hoplite shield (about 34in. in diameter) and wearing a thorax with elongated *pteruges* (leather or linen tabs) – perhaps a *linothorax* – and in the act of making an overhand thrust with what must have been a hoplite spear (*dory*), although the weapon is lost. Although this could be a depiction of a Greek mercenary, his proximity to Alexander suggests rather that he is a member of the hypaspists.

TOP LEFT **Greaves from the so-called Tomb of Philip II in Vergina. The fact that the left greave is shorter than the right one has been attributed to the fact that Philip's leg had been broken in a Triballian campaign. In fact, Philip's injury was to the right leg, and to the thigh bone. (Archaeological Museum, Thessaloniki)**

TOP RIGHT **Phrygian helmet, with lobate crest and no cheek pieces, fourth century BC. This one is from Epirus, but it is of the type used by the infantrymen on the Alexander Sarcophagus. Note the decoration on the crest and the tubular plume holder. (Ioannina Museum, no. 6419)**

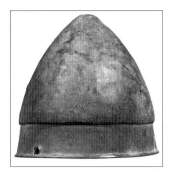

There are reasons for believing that the hypaspists were more mobile and versatile (although many believe this is simply a reflection of age, physique, and training), but certain functions of the hypaspists may have required them to put aside the *sarissa*, or at least to use a considerably shorter one. The reference to hypaspists as 'the lightest troops and best armed' (Arrian, 4.28.8) will mean that they carried the light hoplite spear, just under 8ft in length and weighing slightly over 2lb. One example of a butt spike, after cleaning, revealed the letters 'MAK,' showing that it was standard Macedonian government issue. Hypaspists were used primarily on rough terrain, in siege warfare, and in close, hand-to-hand fighting. In such situations the *sarissa* is at best cumbersome, and at worst useless. In the taking of city walls it would have been difficult for the hypaspists to scale ladders while carrying 18ft *sarissai* and protecting themselves only with the 2ft *pelte*. Although we have a description of Ptolemy at Kamelon Teichos, in the battle at the Nile in 321/0, using the *sarissa* from atop the wall to strike at the enemy elephants, this is a completely different matter. Also, the term *hyperaspizantes* used of hypaspists who held up their shields to protect the king or a comrade implies something larger than the 2ft shield of the *pezhetairoi*.

A killing scene from the Alexander Sarcophagus. This may show the execution of a prisoner. If the victim is still fighting, there are no traces of his offensive and defensive weapons. The victors are either mercenary hoplites or hypaspists, and the killer uses the straight *xiphos*. The scene has been interpreted by many, but for no compelling reason, as the murder of Perdiccas in Egypt. (Archaeological Museum, Istanbul)

CONDITIONS OF SERVICE

As far as we can tell, there were no limits placed on the Macedonian infantryman's term of service. He was called upon to serve when needed, for as long as he was needed. But Alexander's Panhellenic expedition against Persia was exceptional. Allied troops, supplied by the members of the League of Corinth, went to participate in the war of vengeance on Persia, and the king was under moral pressure to release them from service after the fall of the Achaemenid capitals, or at least after the death of Darius III. The Macedonians received no such consideration, nor could they have abandoned the expedition – even with the king's consent – without dishonor, as the mutinies at the Hyphasis and Opis made clear.

Even by ancient standards, the demands made on the Macedonian infantryman were great. Not only was he expected to campaign throughout the year, regardless of the season, but the conquests of Alexander took him from the Balkans to the Indus, across desert wastes and some of the world's highest mountain passes. By the calculations of the author Theodore Ayrault Dodge, the infantryman who campaigned with Alexander in Europe in 336–34 and then joined the Asiatic campaign had covered 20,870 miles by the time Alexander died in Babylon in 323, an average of 1,605 miles per year. For many of the infantrymen this was not the end of it. The argyraspids marched from Cilicia to Egypt and back (if they did not first make a detour to Media) and then campaigned with Eumenes in Mesopotamia, Persia, and on the Iranian plateau, thus adding at least another 5,000 miles to a journey that was destined to leave their bones scattered throughout distant lands. Alexander's route to Bactria and then to India took them twice over mountain passes that approached or exceeded 12,000ft. Many of Alexander's veterans could claim to have crossed the Euphrates and Tigris rivers, the Oxus (Amu-darya) and Iaxartes (Syr-darya), the Indus and three of its tributaries, as well as the Nile. To these natural obstacles, we may add the seemingly impregnable fortresses of Tyre and Gaza, the Rocks of Ariamazes and Sisimithres, and Aornus on the edge of the Indus, all of which combined natural and man-made positions with armed defenders.

Disease and wounds carried off more than the Alexander historians and the king's propagandists cared to admit, and settlements in central Asia were dotted with colonists who included those infantrymen unfit for battle (*apomachoi*). Sometimes their stay was temporary, and they later rejoined the army, but for many it was a bleak and unwelcome 'retirement.'

Pay

The question of pay for Macedonian infantrymen is a particularly difficult one. Certainly in the time of Philip II, the Macedonian phalangites, as a national army (i.e. conscripts) called up for campaigns, received no attested daily or monthly pay, although Philip must have been responsible

BOTTOM LEFT **Bronze butt spike of a spear (*dory*). The letters MAK, abbreviating Makedonon ('of the Macedonians'), were inscribed on it, showing that it was standard government issue. It is presumably of the sort used by Macedonian hypaspists. (Greek Museum, University of Newcastle upon Tyne)**

BOTTOM RIGHT **Persian shield beside a fallen infantryman. This is a detail of the main battle scene on the Alexander Sarcophagus from Sidon. (Archaeological Museum, Istanbul)**

for their daily subsistence. The Macedonian king, however, compensated for the lack of regular pay by allowing the soldiers to plunder cities and despoil their enemies on occasions. It appears that, in the early stages at least, Alexander followed this practice. Plunder is an inducement to those about to do battle, and although in the preliminaries to the battle of Issus Alexander reminds the Illyrians and Thracians specifically that 'the enemy line [is] agleam with gold and purple – equipped with booty not arms' (Curtius Rufus, 3.10.9), the words resounded with all fighting men.

Of course, plunder (or the proceeds of plunder) was awarded in proportion to the service of the individual, and infantrymen were notoriously underpaid in relation to the cavalry. Even amongst the infantry there were those whose portions were greater. After the surrender of Babylon, Alexander amassed so much wealth that he distributed bonuses to the troops: 'The Macedonian cavalry were each given 600 denarii while the foreign cavalry received 500, the Macedonian infantry 200 and the others three months' pay' (Curtius Rufus, 5.1.45). In this passage, from a Roman historian, we should take the denarius to be the equivalent of the drachma (cf. Diodorus of Sicily, 17.64.6: 'he distributed to each of the cavalrymen six minas [= 600 drachmae], to each of the allied cavalrymen five, and to the Macedonians of the phalanx two, and he gave to all the mercenaries two months' pay').

This distribution of spoils raises further questions about the matter of pay for Macedonians themselves. Are the ratios themselves meaningful? If so, then a Macedonian cavalryman earned two-and-a-half times as much as an infantryman (i.e. phalangite). But this can hardly be correct, since we know from the Hellenistic period that infantry officers received between two and four times as much pay as the regular infantryman. It is inconceivable that a junior officer of the infantry would have been paid (whether in wages or bonuses) as much as or more than a cavalryman. Nor does there appear to be a relationship between the size of the bonus and the normal monthly pay – if it existed for Macedonian infantrymen. If we assume that 200 drachmae (or 2 minas) amounted to two months' pay (or even three, if Diodorus' text is to be brought into line with Curtius'), then a phalangite would have earned either 100 or just over 66.5 drachmae per month, that is, either 3.3 or just over 2 drachmas per day. This would be at odds with the commonly accepted – but perhaps false – assumption that at the beginning of Alexander's campaign a hypaspist earned one drachma per day; and it is unlikely that an elite hypaspist would earn less than a *pezhetairos*. Furthermore, Arrian discusses the mixed phalanx in 323 and says:

> The Persians were then enrolled in the various Macedonian units, so that the *dekas* – or section – now consisted of a Macedonian leader, two his compatriots, one of them a dimoirites, the other a 'ten-stater man' (so called from the pay he received, which was less than that of the dimoirites ['double pay man'] but more than that of the ordinary rank and file), twelve Persians, and, last, another Macedonian 'ten-stater man.' (7.23.3–4)

Milns ('Army Pay,' 246–7) has estimated that in the late stages of Alexander's campaign, a 'ten-stater man' may have earned 200 drachmae per month, a *dimoirites* 300, and the average phalangite 150.

Alexander the Great on horseback, from the so-called Alexander Mosaic of Naples. There has been some debate about whether the work shows the battle of Issus or Gaugamela. Behind Alexander one can see a Macedonian cavalryman wearing the Boeotian helmet. To the side of Alexander's horse, behind the king's hand, are traces of the face of an infantryman. (Ann Ronan Picture Library)

The elite hypaspist, we must assume, made more than the average phalangite, though we do not know how much. In all, by Milns' estimate, Alexander was spending the equivalent of the annual income of the empire on the military.

Rewards, promotion, and other forms of recognition

During Alexander's siege of Halicarnassus, which was by its nature primarily a task for infantrymen, the king stationed his best fighters (*promachoi*) in the front ranks, but it is hard to determine whether this means the best units or the men most conspicuous for their valor, drawn from various units. It is, however, worth noting that some of the veterans, who on account of their age were exempt from the most dangerous fighting (Diodorus, 17.27.1), distinguished themselves on this occasion. Their deeds would have been known to all, and those who had not witnessed the events heard their exploits praised throughout the camp. Hence at a drinking party some six years later, the cavalry officer Black Cleitus referred to the bravery of the older warriors:

> You express contempt for Philip's men, but you are forgetting that, if old Atarrhias here had not brought the younger fellows back into line, we should still be delayed around Halicarnassus. (Curtius Rufus, 8.1.36)

Atarrhias and Hellanicus, who are mentioned by Arrian in his account of the siege of Halicarnassus, were promoted to command chiliarchies and pentakosiarchies when such honors were distributed on the basis of valor in Sittacene, not far from Babylon, in 331 BC. The selection of officers (that is, for the *hegemones* but not the *strategoi* or the *archihyhpaspistes*) on the basis of valor may have been standard practice amongst the regular hypaspists. The royal hypaspists, too, showed no shortage of valor, and the most notable of them, Peucestas, who saved Alexander's life in the Mallian town in India, was made an exceptional eighth *somatophylax* (i.e. a member of the elite bodyguard) as a result. He did not retain the office long, since he was soon appointed satrap of Persia, but the gesture was significant and must have amounted to something greater than the Victoria Cross or the Medal of Honor.

It has been argued by some that not only individuals but actual units were recognized as the 'best' (*aristoi*) and occupied positions of honor in the battle-line. Hence it had been supposed that the *taxeis* designated as *asthetairoi* were those considered the 'best companions' (*aristoi* + *hetairoi*). This is an attractive theory, but it has very little to support it. In fact, those *taxeis* that are called *asthetairoi* seem to be the same throughout the campaign. Furthermore, the *taxis* of Craterus, who was the commander of the infantry on the left and clearly the senior taxiarch, is never designated as 'the best.' As is suggested above, the *asthetairoi* appear to have been named for their position in the battle-line rather than their military prowess.

Other forms of recognition included the payment of bonuses and the distribution of plunder. After the first campaigning season in Asia, Alexander allowed the newly wed soldiers to spend the winter of 334/3 with their wives in Macedonia, but as the campaign progressed such leaves became impractical. For those who died in battle, too, there were the honors of military funerals and stipends paid to their widows and children. It is noteworthy, however, that commemorative statues like those crafted by Lysippus for the fallen at the Granicus were reserved for cavalrymen (Arrian, 1.16.7; cf. Plutarch, *Alexander* 16.16, who wrongly includes nine *pezhetairoi*) and in general the funerals of the officers and common soldiers were conducted separately (Plutarch, *Eumenes* 9.5). In 324, the king paid all the debts of those who were about to be discharged, the total cost of which was 9,870 talents (Plutarch, *Alexander* 70). One of the benefits of conquering an empire as wealthy as that of the Persians was that Alexander had the resources to be generous with his troops, both the living and the dead.

Punishment

The discipline imposed upon the Macedonian phalangite was certainly harsher than that employed by 'democratic' armies, where citizen soldiers had legal recourse against the perceived abuses of their elected officers (Hamel, *Athenian Generals* 118–21). In Macedonia, the ultimate authority rested with the king, and it was he who regulated the conduct of his officers. Officers themselves could be punished, as we have seen, for bathing in warm water or for bringing flute-girls into camp against the king's orders. The rules of conduct were the same, if not more severe, for the infantrymen.

The Alexander historians say little about punishment for minor offences, though it appears that flogging, which was used against the pages Hermolaus and Aphthonetus, was a standard form of corporal punishment; if it was used to discipline young noblemen, it must certainly have been applied generously to commoners for even lesser forms of misconduct. In Greek armies, soldiers guilty of insubordination were required to stand at attention in full armor for an extended period, and this too was used by the Macedonians – in the case of one of Philip's pages, a man named Archedamus (Aelian, *Varia Historia* 14.48), who in the next stage of his career would have become a royal hypaspist – although in the case of the *pezhetairoi*, especially if they lacked breastplates, this could hardly have been onerous. Others may simply have been moved to disciplinary units, *ataktoi*, where the demands made of them were greater and their behavior was closely monitored.

Other regulations clearly existed for the protection of property, including the women who had become attached to the army. Although rape was a standard feature of the looting and destruction of an enemy city or camp, the women who had been carried off as booty or those of the camp-followers who had become, in effect, the common-law wives of soldiers, were treated as personal property. Plutarch comments on a notorious case:

> When Alexander discovered that Damon and Timotheus, two Macedonian soldiers who were serving under Parmenion, had seduced the wives of some of the Greek mercenaries, he sent orders to Parmenion that if the two men were found guilty, they should be put to death as wild beasts who are born to prey upon mankind. (Plutarch, *Alexander*, 22)

For dress-code violations or failure to maintain equipment properly, we have evidence of a system of fines used in the time of Philip V:

> … they shall punish according to the written rules those who are not bearing arms appropriate to them: two obols for the kottybos, the same amount for the konos, three obols for the sarissa, the same amount for the dagger [machaira], two obols for the greaves, a drachma for the shield. In the case of officers double the fine for the weapons mentioned, and two drachmas for the corselet and one drachma for the half-corselet. (Austin, no. 74)

This is the frontispiece of Rollin's *History of Greece* (vol. 2, 1849). It shows Timocleia being brought before Alexander. She was the sister of Theagenes the Theban (perhaps a member of the Sacred Band) who died at Chaeronea. Timocleia herself was a victim of rape, but she threw her attacker into a well. She was acquitted by Alexander not because her cause was just but because of her family background and the dignity of her bearing.

The *konos* is a type of helmet, but the word *kottybos* is not found elsewhere. It appears to be a variant form of *kossymbos* (–ss– often substitutes for –tt–, e.g. *thalassa* and *thalatta* both mean 'sea'; cf. 'Arymbas' as a variant form of the name Arybbas), which is a type of cloak.

Serious offences were punishable by death, by stoning or javelins, or in a more dramatic way in the case of mutineers. Two examples suffice. The first involves the ringleaders of the mutiny at Opis in 324. Arrian, who is less critical of Alexander than the other extant historians, says:

> Alexander leapt from the platform with the officers who attended him, and pointing with his finger to the ringleaders of the mutiny, ordered the guards

[*hypaspistai*] to arrest them. There were thirteen of them, and they were marched off to execution. (7.8.3)

The form of their punishment is spelled out by Quintus Curtius Rufus:

Alexander repeated the command, since those previously ordered had momentarily hesitated: the prisoners were to be hurled into the river [i.e. the Tigris], still in their chains. (10.4.2)

In the second case, those who had mutinied against their officers at the time of Alexander's death were treated to an even more cruel form of punishment:

Perdiccas withdrew from the main body [of the infantry] some 300 men who had followed Meleager at the time when he first burst from the meeting after Alexander's death, and before the eyes of the entire army he threw them to the elephants. All were trampled to death beneath the feet of the beasts. (Quintus Curtius Rufus, 10.9.18–19)

ON CAMPAIGN, IN THE CAMP, AND ON THE MARCH

The camp

Several passages written by the Alexander historians record the severe conditions that soldiers on the march were forced to endure, through deserts, mountain passes, and jungle, but there are few details about the conditions of the individual soldier. We know that they slept in tents – except in special circumstances, like the Indian campaign, where fear of poisonous snakes forced them to devise 'hammocks' suspended from the trees – since we have references to waterproof tent-covers that were filled with straw and stitched together to form rafts on which the men and their baggage could cross rivers. Furthermore, Arrian 4.19.1 mentions iron tent-pegs. Just as Alexander had his *stromatophylax* ('guardian of the household equipment'), so the individual *dekas* had its own slave who was responsible for the communal baggage, normally transported on some pack-animal. Like the Roman *contubernium*, the *dekas* was the basic unit that stayed together on the march and shared living quarters, though we do not know how many shared a single tent. Diodorus' description of a camp built at the Hyphasis to deceive posterity is of limited help:

Here he dug a ditch fifty feet wide and forty feet deep, and throwing up the earth on the inside constructed out of it a substantial wall. He directed the infantry to construct huts each containing two beds five cubits [i.e. $7\frac{1}{2}$ft] long. (17.95.1–2)

Although Alexander was creating a camp of exaggerated proportions, the basic layout may nevertheless be correct. The camp was surrounded by a defensive trench and an interior wall (Arrian, 3.9.1; cf. Curtius

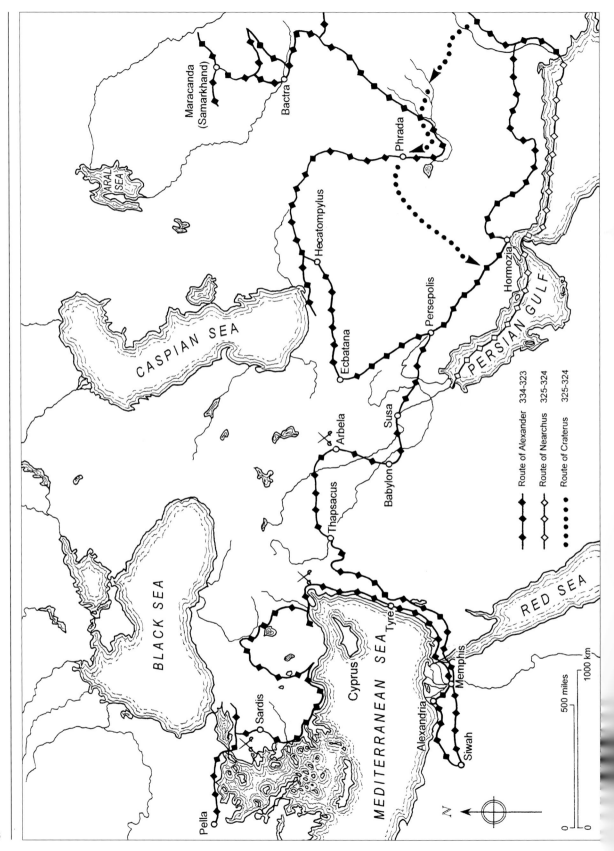

Route of Alexander 334-323
Route of Nearchus 325-324
Route of Craterus 325-324

Maracanda (Samarkhand)
Bactra
Phrada
ARAL SEA
Hecatompylus
Hormozia
Persepolis
PERSIAN GULF
Ecbatana
CASPIAN SEA
Susa
Arbela
Babylon
Thapsacus
BLACK SEA
MEDITERRANEAN SEA
Tyre
RED SEA
Cyprus
Memphis
Sardis
Alexandria
Siwah
Pella

N

500 miles
1000 km

26

Rufus, 4.12.24), and the number of men per tent may have been two, or at most four. Diodorus says that in the time of the Successors, Eumenes constructed a false camp, intended to mislead his enemy:

> He ordered all the commanders to follow him with their own soldiers bringing fire in many jars. He then selected a place in the higher ground that faced toward the desert and was well situated to be clearly visible from every direction and by setting up markers laid out a space with a perimeter of seventy stades [roughly 8 miles]. Assigning an area to each of those who followed him, he ordered them at night to light fires about twenty cubits [30 feet] apart and to keep the flames bright in the first watch as if men were still awake and busy with the care of their bodies and the preparation of food, but dimmer in the second watch, and in the third watch to leave only a few. (19.38.3; cf. Polyaenus, *Stratagemata*, 4.8.4)

A camp of this size was meant to reflect the size of the actual army: in this case there were 36,000 infantry, 6,700 cavalry (and their horses) and 116 elephants. We have no figures for the numbers of non-combatants. But the reference to one fire every 30ft suggests that half a file may have shared a campfire: four tents, measuring about 6ft in width and holding two men each, and separated by about 2ft, would total exactly 30ft. If the other half-file pitched their tents on the other side of the fire, one fire could serve an entire *dekas*.

Lines of supply and communication

Supplies and provisions were normally purchased en route, either in friendly villages or from caravans of merchants who followed the army to make their living. Many of the debts incurred by the common Macedonians were the result of interactions with these caravans, which offered the attractions of prostitution and gambling. Beggars and thieves must have made their rounds as well. The official baggage train of the army increased steadily as well, and the accumulated booty included slaves and concubines, and ultimately large numbers of illegitimate children. At the end of the campaign, Alexander legitimized such unions at Susa, celebrating the marriages of some 10,000 of his veterans. It was the camp-followers who suffered the most on the difficult marches, and formed a high percentage of those who perished in the infamous Gedrosian disaster of 325 BC. In such situations the pack-animals did double duty as 'food on the hoof,' but the slaughter of such beasts also meant the abandoning of baggage, not all of it non-essential. Quintus Curtius Rufus describes the conditions of the Gedrosian march:

> Their provisions exhausted, the Macedonians began to experience first shortage of food and eventually starvation. They rummaged about for palm roots (that being the only tree growing there) but, when even this means of sustenance ran out, they began to slaughter their pack-animals, sparing not even their horses. Then, having nothing to carry their baggage, they proceeded to burn the spoils they had taken from the enemy, spoils for which they had

penetrated the furthest reaches of the East. (9.10.11–12)

For the soldier on the march there were also benefits to campaigning in the Persian Empire. Its infrastructure, especially its system of royal roads, made movement and communication relatively easy. No matter where the Macedonian army went, it appears to have maintained its lines of communication and received a steady flow of reinforcements and supplies. Individuals were thus able to send home and receive letters, though the turn-around period must have been considerable.

In addition to the opportunities for looting, the troops were treated to periods of 'R and R,' and the expedition was joined in several places by troupes of actors and artists. Athletic and artistic competitions are attested, and there were doubtless numerous activities in which the infantrymen themselves could participate, although hardly the glamorous pursuits of the aristocracy, who engaged in the hunting of exotic animals. In some cases they were content to enjoy the antics of the camp-followers:

> The camp-followers, in sport, had divided themselves up into two bands, and set a general and commander over each of them, one of whom they called Alexander, and the other Darius; and they had begun by pelting one another with clods of earth, then had fought with their fists, and finally, heated with the desire of battle, had taken stones and sticks, being now many and hard to quell. (Plutarch, *Alexander*, 31.3–4)

The scene calls to mind the 'Tafurs' of the First Crusade, and incidents of this sort, perhaps not always harmless, must have been common enough.

Physical and emotional impact

What was life like for the individual, and how did the warrior himself endure the burdens of the campaign? These are things that, in other ages, can be learned from letters written to loved ones at home, or testimony given at courts martial. For the veteran of Alexander's campaigns we must turn to the speech of the taxiarch (now promoted to hipparch) Coenus son of Polemocrates delivered at the Hyphasis River. From this we learn of the cumulative effects, physical and moral, of the lengthy campaign:

> Whatever mortals were capable of, we have achieved. We have crossed lands and seas, all of them now better known to us than to their inhabitants. We stand almost at the end of the earth [and]

The stag hunt on a mosaic from Pella (*c*.300 BC). (Archaeological Museum of Pella, Ann Ronan Picture Library)

you are preparing to enter another world ... That is a programme appropriate to your spirit, but beyond ours. For your valor will ever be on the increase, but our energy is already running out. Look at our bodies – debilitated, pierced with all those wounds, decaying with all their scars! Our weapons are blunt; our armour is wearing out ... How many of us have a cuirass? Who owns a horse? Have an inquiry made into how many are attended by slaves and what anyone has left of his booty. Conquerors of all, we lack everything! And our problems result not from extravagance; no, on war have we expended the equipment of war. (Quintus Curtius Rufus, 9.3.7–11)

Bacchanalian behavior

Finally, it is worth mentioning an incident that many apologists for Alexander regard as fictitious: the Bacchic revel in Carmania. In the light of the miseries experienced by the army in India (described above) and on the march through Baluchistan, and in view of the fact that the empire was now securely in Alexander's hands, the Carmanian interlude strikes the reader as perfectly understandable. Plutarch's account is as follows:

> The march [through Carmania] soon developed into a kind of Bacchanalian procession. Alexander himself feasted continually, day and night, reclining with his Companions on a dais built upon a high and conspicuous rectangular platform, the whole structure being slowly drawn along by eight horses. Innumerable wagons followed the royal table, some of them covered with purple or embroidered canopies, others shaded by the boughs of trees, which were constantly kept fresh and green: these vehicles carried the rest of Alexander's officers, all of them crowned with flowers and drinking wine. Not a single helmet, shield or spear was to be seen, but the whole line of the march the soldiers kept dipping their cups, drinking-horns or earthenware goblets into huge casks and mixing-bowls and toasting one another, some drinking as they marched, others sprawled by the wayside, while the whole landscape resounded with the music of pipes and flutes, with harping and singing and the cries of women rapt with the divine frenzy. Not only drinking but all the other forms of bacchanalian license attended this straggling and disorderly march. (Plutarch, *Alexander*, 67)

This, too, was the Macedonian army, and 'membership had its privileges.'

ORGANIZATION, NUMBERS, AND TERMINOLOGY

The Macedonian phalangites can be subdivided into two main groups: the regional 'heavy infantry,' known as the *pezhetairoi* or *pezetairoi* ('foot companions'), and the elite infantry guard, the *hypaspistai* or hypaspists (literally, 'shield bearers'). Within the *pezhetairoi* there were troops designated as *asthetairoi* – the meaning of which has been the subject of considerable debate – and within the hypaspists there were those who were distinguished by the adjective 'royal' (*basilikoi*). In terms of equipment, the *pezhetairoi* and *asthetairoi* were identical, but it is virtually certain that the hypaspists were not armed in the same way as the *pezhetairoi*.

When Alexander crossed into Asia in 334, he took with him 12,000 Macedonian phalangites: 9,000 of these were *pezhetairoi*, divided into six units (*taxis*, plural: *taxeis*), each 1,500 strong, which modern scholars have variously described as 'battalions' or 'brigades.' In addition to these there were 3,000 hypaspists, who may have been from the very start of the campaign assigned to 1,000-man units called chiliarchies, although it is possible that the chiliarchy structure was not imposed until 331 and that earlier references to chiliarchs (i.e. the commanders) and chiliarchies are anachronistic.

At Thebes in 335, Alexander's army comprised 30,000 infantry, but these must have included allied troops – certainly the Boeotian troops who yearned for the destruction of the city – and mercenaries. For the protection of the homeland, and to deal with uprisings by the Greeks, the regent Antipater was left with 12,000 infantry, of whom some must have been hypaspists. Alexander made regular demands on Macedonian manpower throughout the campaign, but Antipater amassed a force of 40,000 infantry to deal with Agis III in 331; at least half of these must have been of Macedonian peasant stock. In 323, when the outbreak of the Lamian War left Macedonia denuded of allies, Antipater marched south through Thessaly with 13,000 Macedonian infantry.

Pezhetairoi

There has been a great deal of debate concerning the formation of the *pezhetairoi* and the name itself. Theopompus (born *c.*378 BC), a historian who was contemporary with Philip II and Alexander, said that 'the largest and most powerful men were specially chosen (*epilektoi*) from all the Macedonians and served as the king's bodyguard and were called *pezhetairoi*' (FGrH 115 F 348). This is also reflected in the Second Olynthiac of the Athenian orator, Demosthenes, who says that Philip's best troops were mercenaries (*xenoi*) and *pezhetairoi*. But it soon becomes clear that the troops Theopompus and Demosthenes are speaking of are those who, at least in Alexander's time, were known as hypaspists. And one other contemporary historian, whose work, like that of Theopompus, survives only in fragments, says that King Alexander

> called the notables [i.e. the aristocracy] who were accustomed to ride with the king 'companion' [*hetairoi*], and the majority, that is, the infantry, he divided into *lochoi* and *dekades* and other units and called them *pezhetairoi* in order that both would share in the 'companionship' of the King and would perform their tasks more eagerly. (FGrH 72 F4)

Despite the ongoing debate over the identity of 'King Alexander,' the only plausible interpretation is that we are dealing with Alexander the Great, and that the extension of the name *pezhetairoi* to the heavy infantry was accompanied by a name-change that saw the former *pezhetairoi* become the hypaspists.

Asthetairoi

Some scholars have seen the *asthetairoi* as a separate group of Macedonian phalangites, and various interpretations of the prefix 'asth–' have been put forward. It may come from 'asty,' which means 'city' – or, more precisely, from *astoi*, meaning 'townsmen' – but the *taxeis* that are referred to as *asthetairoi* appear to come from Upper Macedonia, where cities are in short supply. Others have suggested *aristoi* (= 'the best'), and noted that the *asthetairoi* seem to have been located in a position of honor on the right side of the infantry line, next to the hypaspists. But the prevailing view is that *asthetairoi* means 'closest companions' (in terms of 'closest in kinship') and designates those *taxeis* from Upper Macedonia. The author's own guess is that it does mean 'closest,' but in a spatial sense. These were the *taxeis* that were known to fight in a position 'closest' to the king. Whether they were located there because they were 'best' is possible, but it would be odd to find the great phalanx commander Craterus located on the far left if the right was the position of excellence. The *asthetairoi* may have been better equipped or trained to fight next to the hypaspists.

Hypaspistai (regular hypaspists)

The hypaspists were clearly an elite force, and almost certainly more mobile than the *pezhetairoi*. In the major battles they acted as a link

Hypaspist, with hoplite shield, *linothorax* and greaves, depicted in hand-to-hand struggle on the Alexander Sarcophagus of Sidon. The scene appears to depict the fighting at Gaugamela (331 BC). (Archaeological Museum, Istanbul)

A: The phalangite (*pezhetairos*)

A

B: *Pezhetairoi* in training

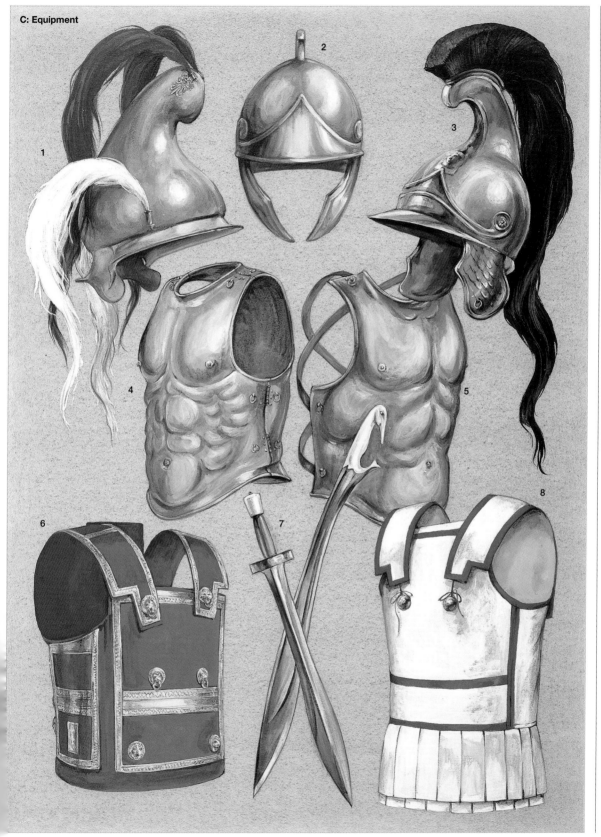

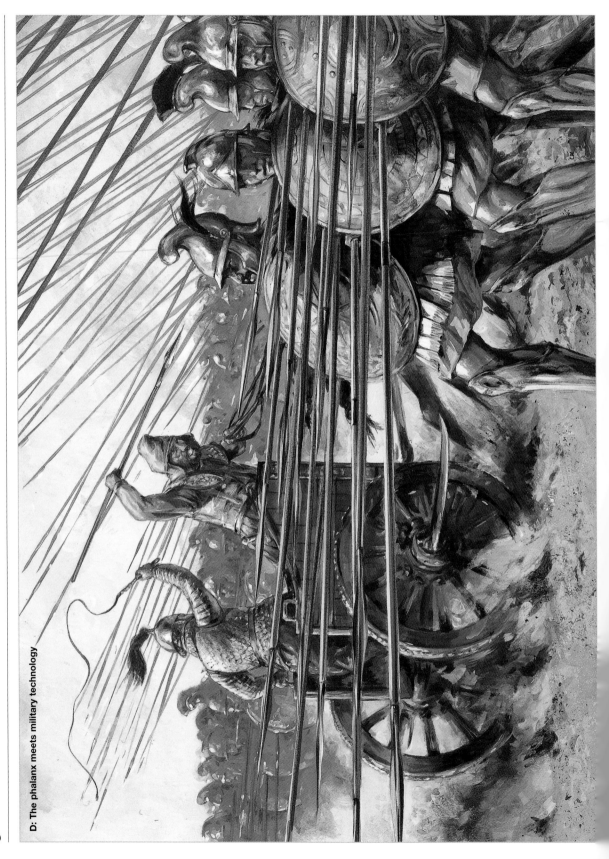

D: The phalanx meets military technology

E: Reality – the weakness of the phalangite in hand-to-hand fighting

E

F: Campaigning: hypaspists and *pezhetairoi* on broken ground, the Thracian campaign of 336/5 BC

F

G: The aftermath of battle

H: The elite infantryman, the hypaspist

between the heavy infantry and the cavalry. They were taken by the king on special missions that involved speed and endurance, often fighting in rugged areas. Named for their shields – and indeed the hypaspist veterans formed the so-called argyraspids or 'silver shields' – they were the infantry guard and, of all the infantry troops, they fought closest to the king. Small detachments of hypaspists acted as guards at official events and banquets, and also as a police force. For example, it was a detachment of hypaspists led by Atarrhias that went to arrest Philotas in 330 BC; during the Cleitus episode, when the king felt threatened, he called for the hypaspists; and he used the same force to arrest the mutineers at Opis in 324. There is a strong likelihood that, on occasion at least, they were armed more like traditional Greek hoplites and they are often referred to, loosely, as *doryphoroi* ('spear-bearers'). Although they had unit-commanders, chiliarchs and pentakosiarchs, the entire force was under the command of the *archihypaspistes* (literally, 'the leader of the hypaspists'). Between 334 and 330 this was Nicanor son of Parmenion; his successor may have been Neoptolemus, one of the Aeacidae and thus a relative of Olympias, the mother of Alexander the Great.

Argyraspids

Literally the 'silver shields,' the argyraspids were named for the decoration of their armor. The unit had its origins in Alexander's regular hypaspists, and already in the accounts of Gaugamela, Diodorus and Curtius Rufus (following the same source) anachronistically refer to the hypaspists as argyraspids. Both units numbered 3,000 and their

Detail from the Alexander Mosaic showing the face of what is probably a royal hypaspist, fighting as a *hamippos*. The oft-repeated observation that he may be an officer of the hypaspists is less likely to be true. (National Museum, Naples, Ann Ronan Picture Library)

distinguishing characteristic was their shields. In fact, Diodorus says that 'the infantry unit of the argyraspids [was] distinguished by the brilliance of its arms and the bravery of its men' (17.57.2). Hence it is likely that their shields were not simply decorated but of a larger size than those of the *pezhetairoi*. The commander of argyraspids, Antigenes, is the same man who came second in the contest of valor at Sittacene in 330, and the nine officers appointed on that occasion were almost certainly hypaspist commanders. In the time of the Successors, the argyraspids spoke of themselves as a unit that had not known defeat in Alexander's lifetime and as men who were advanced in age, victorious veterans who had been dismissed in 324 but prevented by the turmoil that accompanied the king's death from reaching home and enjoying the fruits of a well-deserved retirement. In 318, they joined Eumenes in the war against Antigonus the One-Eyed, and although they fought with distinction at Paraetacene and Gabiene in the following year they surrendered their commander to the enemy in exchange for their wives and baggage, which had been captured in the latter battle.

Hypaspistai basilikoi (royal hypaspists)

The main difference between the regular and royal hypaspists was that the latter were clearly of aristocratic background, and most, if not all, were formerly members of the *paides basilikoi* or 'royal pages' (they are sometimes called the 'royal cohort' by Roman authors). We do not know how numerous the royal hypaspists were or exactly how they fought in major battles. During the storming of city walls they are found in the immediate vicinity of the king, and if they stayed close to the king on the battlefield they may have operated as *hamippoi*, interspersed among the horsemen. There is no clear evidence for this in a set-piece battle – although on the Alexander Mosaic from Naples traces of such an infantryman can be seen near the rear of Alexander's horse – but Curtius Rufus describes an incident in 328 in which:

> The King, frequently changing horses, pressed the retreating enemy relentlessly. The young noblemen who formed his usual retinue had given up the chase, all except Philip, the brother of Lysimachus, who was in the early stages of manhood and, as was readily apparent, was a person of rare qualities. Incredibly, Philip kept up with the King on foot although Alexander rode for over 500 stades ... Philip could not be induced to leave the King, even though he was wearing a cuirass and carrying weapons. On reaching a wood where the barbarians had hidden, this same young man put up a remarkable fight and gave protection to the King when engaged in hand-to-hand combat with the enemy. (Curtius Rufus, 8.2.35–37)

The case of Philip shows an aristocratic youth, fighting in a 'royal cohort' (i.e. the king's 'usual retinue') in a role similar to that of the *hamippoi*.

The known commanders of royal hypaspists are Admetus (probably) Hephaestion (possibly), and Seleucus (certainly). Of these, Hephaestion was wounded at Gaugamela by a cavalryman's lance (*xyston*), that is, in the thick of the action. As commander of this group, he may himself have been mounted.

Taxeis and chiliarchia

The details of Macedonian military organization come mainly from writers of the first century BC (i.e. almost 300 years after Philip II and Alexander) and later: Asclepiodotus (perhaps recording nothing more than notes taken from his teacher Poseidonius); Aelian the Tactician; an Arrian (from the *Tactica*). Their details are not easily reconciled with those of the extant Alexander historians. By the late third and early second centuries, it appears that a *lochos* numbered 16, and four *lochoi* formed a tetrarchy. Four tetrarchies then made up a *syntagma*. But the organization and terminology in Alexander's time was clearly much different. Furthermore, the tactical writers do not supply historical examples and often present theory instead of actual practise.

It appears that in Alexander's time the basic unit was the *dekas* (plural: *dekades*), a file, nominally of ten men but soon extended to 16. Sixteen such files (16 x 16) formed a *lochos* (later known as a *syntagma*) of 256, under the command of a *lochagos* (cf. Milns, 'Hypaspists,' 195; but Sekunda, *Alexander's Army*, 37 assumes that a *lochos* comprised 512); the individual member of a *lochos* was known as a *lochites* (Arrian, 3.9.6). Thus the strength of the *taxis* was probably six *lochoi* (= 1,536) and that of a chiliarchy was four *lochoi* (= 1024). Half a chiliarchy would be a pentakosiarchy (512 men). The size of the *lochos* made the relaying of commands more difficult, for, according to Asclepiodotus (*Tactics* 2.9), in a unit of 64 (8 x 8), the men could easily hear all the commands, but with the doubling of the file-size and the creation of squares 16 x 16, it became necessary to add supernumeraries or *ektaktoi*. There were five of these: a herald (*stratokêrux*), a signalman (*sêmeiophoros*), a bugler (*salpingtês*), an aide (*hypêretês*), and a file-closer (*ouragos*). The general (*strategos*) who served as the *taxiarches* was almost certainly stationed behind the *taxis* and on horseback, from which position he sent orders to the various *ektaktoi* whose job it was to distribute the orders. Each *taxis* of *pezhetairoi* (1,500 men) would thus have had 30 supernumeraries.

The lowest-ranking officer in Alexander's infantry actually identified by name – excluding Habreas the *dimoirites*, who died under exceptional circumstances, defending Alexander in the Mallian campaign – is the chiliarch, although we appear to have the names of three chiliarchs and six pentakosiarchs in a passage in Quintus Curtius Rufus (5.2.5): Atarrhias, Antigenes, Philotas the Augaean, Amyntas, Antigonus, Amyntas Lyncestes, Theodorus, and Hellanicus, and one individual whose name is lost from the list.

Commanders of the *pezhetairoi* (334–31)

Position	Battle of Granicus 334	Battle of Issus 333	Battle of Gaugamela 331
1 right	Perdiccas	Coenus	Coenus
2	Coenus	Perdiccas	Perdiccas
3	Amyntas	Meleager	Meleager
4	Philip	Ptolemy [Philip]	Polyperchon [Philip/Ptolemy]
5	Meleager	Amyntas	Simmias [Amyntas]
6 left	Craterus	Craterus	Craterus

Commanders of the *pezhetairoi* (330–25)

330	329	328	327	326	325
Coenus	Coenus	Coenus	Peithon	Peithon	?
Perdiccas	Alcetas	Alcetas	Alcetas	Alcetas	Alcetas
Amyntas	Attalus	Attalus	Attalus	Attalus	Attalus
Polyperchon	Polyperchon	Polyperchon	Polyperchon	Polyperchon	Polyperchon
Meleager	Meleager	Meleager	Meleager	Meleager	Meleager
Craterus	Craterus	Craterus	Gorgias	Gorgias	Gorgias
			Cleitus	Cleitus	Cleitus

Possible division of hypaspist command in 331

Officer	First chiliarchy	Second chiliarchy	Third chiliarchy
Chiliarch	Atarrhias	Antigenes	Philotas Augaeus
Pentakosiarch	Amyntas	Antigonus	Amyntas Lyncestes
Pentakosiarch	Theodotus	Hellanicus	?

Archihypaspistai and commanders of 'royal hypaspists'

Year	*Archihypaspistes*	Royal hypaspist commander
334	Nicanor	Ptolemy?
333	Nicanor	Admetus
332	Nicanor	Hephaestion
331	Nicanor	Hephaestion
330	Nicanor/Neoptolemus	Hephaestion/Seleucus
329	Neoptolemus	Seleucus
328	Neoptolemus	Seleucus
327	Neoptolemus	Seleucus
326	Neoptolemus	Seleucus
325	Neoptolemus	Seleucus
324	Neoptolemus	Seleucus
323	Neoptolemus	Seleucus

THE PHALANX IN BATTLE

Deployment

It was Alexander's practise to place the Macedonian infantry in the center of his line. On the far right he stationed himself with the companion cavalry, but he used as an articulating force the more mobile hypaspists, 3,000 men stationed immediately to the left of the companions. They formed a link between the cavalry and the heavy infantry. To the left of the hypaspists were stationed first the units known colloquially as the *asthetairoi*, and then the remainder of the *pezhetairoi*. The smaller unit of *hypaspistai basilikoi*, as suggested above, probably worked in tandem with the cavalry and served as *hamippoi* in the actual battle. Hence it is not surprising to find Hephaestion, the commander of

the *somatophylakes* (that is, the *hypaspistai basilikoi*) among the wounded on the right wing at Gaugamela. Other notables who were wounded on the right wing were Menidas, whose cavalry was assigned the task of preventing an outflanking maneuver by the enemy, and Coenus, whose first battalion of *asthetairoi* was positioned closest to the hypaspists.

On the left, adjoining the battalion of Craterus, were the allied and mercenary troops, protected on the wing by the Thessalian cavalry. These were equal in number to the Macedonian companions, and the entire left was, until 330, under the command of Parmenion. At Chaeronea, Alexander had indeed commanded the left, and during the European campaigns – against the so-called 'autonomous' Thracians and at Pellium – he is still found there. But once Alexander began to lead from the right, our knowledge of battles and the contributions of the infantry are generally those that describe the phalanx and hypaspists in relation to Alexander's striking force.

Despite this general division of labor amongst Alexander's troops, the experiences of the *pezhetairoi* in the four major battles – Granicus, Issus, Gaugamela, and the Hydaspes – were very different, largely because of the nature of the terrain, but also because of the enemy's dispositions. Hence it will be useful to consider the role of the Macedonian infantry in each engagement.

The Granicus River

The Granicus was an unusual battle by any standards, but the Persian decision to station their cavalry in the front, and on the steep bank of the river – leaving the numerous Greek mercenary infantry in the rear and unable to affect the outcome of the battle – forced the infantry to move from an inferior position through uneven and treacherous terrain. The banks of the river were sheer in places and the river itself swollen, though yet fordable. But the battle was decided primarily by the cavalry on both sides, with hypaspists attached to the forces of Amyntas son of Arrhabaeus, who commanded the

Figure showing the phalanx in formation from T. A. Dodge's *Alexander* (1890).

Figures from a relief showing the struggle between Macedonian and Persian warriors, from the Alexander Sarcophagus. (The Alexander Sarcophagus, Istanbul Museum)

lancers, and those of Alexander himself. *Pezhetairoi* who entered the river after the initial thrust took place on the right may have used their *sarissai* to dislodge their opponents from the riverbank, but by this time the battle had all but been decided. After the flight of the enemy cavalry and lightly armed troops, the phalanx was used to finish off the Greek mercenaries, who were now abandoned and outflanked. Not surprisingly, Arrian records only about 30 infantrymen killed in the entire battle. And although this has been questioned by some as too low a figure, it doubtless reflects the limited action seen by the infantry in the initial stages and the hopelessness of the situation for the Greek mercenaries in the denouement of the battle.

The battles of Issus and Gaugamela

Far more challenging for the Macedonian infantry was the battle of Issus, where the *pezhetairoi* assumed their usual position in the center, and the hypaspists were drawn up just to their right, on a battlefield broken by the shallow stream of the Pinarus River. The enemy had placed their Greek mercenaries opposite the Macedonian infantry, to the number of 30,000, with 30,000 Persian *kardakes* on either side. Furthermore they had fortified their position by placing *abatis* in the more level areas. When the cavalry on the Macedonian right surged ahead, driving back the Persians on the left and threatening Darius himself in the center, the hypaspists followed and a gap appeared in the middle of the *pezhetairoi* formation. Here they were hard pressed by the Greek mercenaries and suffered their most serious casualties, among them the taxiarch Ptolemy son of Seleucus. In all, some 120 Macedonians of note perished in this stage of the battle, before the Thessalian and allied cavalry had held the Persian onslaught near the sea (on the Macedonian left) and Alexander and the companion cavalry had turned Darius in flight, which signaled the end of the Persian hopes at Issus.

At Gaugamela in 331, on the northern Mesopotamian plains beyond the Tigris, a similar gap occurred in the Macedonian infantry, though somewhat more to the left of center. In this case, however, the impact was not as great, for the opening was exploited by the Persian cavalry, who rushed to the baggage camp. These were soon confronted by the

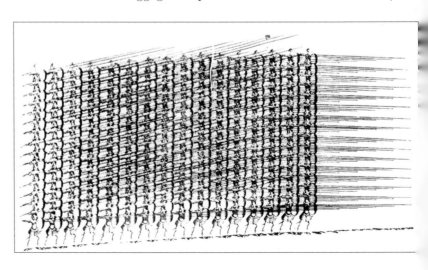

A 17th-century engraving showing the phalanx. (Bibliothèque Nationale, Paris)

Macedonian horse under Menidas. In general, the role of the infantry was to fix the Persian center, while Alexander rolled up the right wing, which he did again with spectacular success, despite the Persian attempts to outflank him.

The battle of the Hydaspes (326 BC)

Like the contest at Gaugamela, the Hydaspes battle was primarily a cavalry contest. The *taxeis* of *pezhetairoi* were deployed in two places along the western bank of the Hydaspes (or Jhelum) River, one force with Craterus immediately opposite the main camp of Porus, and the other with Gorgias, Attalus, and Meleager further upstream. Those infantry who crossed with Alexander some 17 miles upstream in an attempt to outflank the Indian army included the hypaspists (i.e. Antigenes' forces), the *taxis* of White Cleitus and perhaps that of Peithon (formerly Coenus' battalion). At least two *taxeis*, those of Alcetas and Polyperchon, must have remained with Craterus. It has been suggested that after Alexander's crossing upstream, and the failure of Spitaces to prevent it, the *taxeis* of Meleager, Attalus, and Gorgias crossed a midway point on the river (Fuller, *Generalship* 191), but this cannot be substantiated. The victory belonged to the cavalry, but the infantry must have played an important role in neutralizing Porus' elephants.

Experience

The experience of battle for infantrymen normally occurred in one of two forms: set contests on a battlefield selected, or at least accepted, by the commander, and sieges. In the latter case, the *sarissa*-bearing phalangite must have played a secondary role, and it is not surprising that descriptions of the critical stages of taking a city or fortress involve references to the hypaspists or their commanders.

In preparation for a set-piece battle, it was the commander's responsibility to see to it that troops were rested, fed, and put into the best frame of mind for the coming engagement. His own duties included conducting the customary pre-battle sacrifices. Although some generals were influenced by unfavorable omens to postpone or even avoid battle (numerous examples can be found in Xenophon's *Anabasis* and *Hellenica*), others could be blatantly dishonest in their interpretation or manipulation of 'divine signs,' including Alexander himself:

> Alexander of Macedon on one occasion, when about to make sacrifice, used a preparation to inscribe certain letters on the hand which the priest was to place beneath the vitals. These letters indicated that victory was vouchsafed to Alexander. When the steaming liver had received the impress of these characters and had been displayed by the king to the soldiers, the circumstances raised their spirits, since they thought that the god gave them the assurance of victory. (Frontinus, *Stratagems*, 1.11.14)

One should not downplay the role of the supernatural in the events preceding battle (see Pritchett, *Greek State at War*, Part III); indeed, Greek hoplite armies normally engaged only when both sides had received favorable omens. Even the slightest unusual occurrence could disrupt morale, and the fears of the few infected the many. The lengthy exhortations that the historians attribute to Alexander before battle were probably delivered in the camp before the actual deployment of the troops. Whatever the general told them once on the battlefield, it must have been short and to the point, and most of it relayed to the troops by heralds or unit commanders. As far as the troops themselves were concerned, their ability to control and channel their emotions before battle will have depended entirely on the experience and psychological makeup of the individual. What Athenian comic poets said in the Classical period about tunics 'dyed brown' with excrement will have been applicable to Macedonian armies as well, and loss of control of bodily functions, which has been a feature of warfare from the earliest to the most recent times, was a problem even for Alexander's invincible conquerors.

Once in formation, the phalanx sought to overawe the opponent, with visual displays – the gleam of bronze and polished metal, the bristling of the *sarissai* and the undulations of plumes and horsehair crests – and with sounds designed to encourage friend and terrorize foe. Their visual impact on the Persian or Indian enemy will have been the same as that engendered in a Roman general a century and a half later:

> When Aemilius saw how solid a line the Macedonians formed with their interlocking shields and how fiercely they attacked, he was astounded and filled with fear; he had never seen a more terrifying spectacle, and often in later times he used to recall the sight and the feelings it aroused in him. (Plutarch, *Aemilius Paullus*, 19)

As the commander rode in front of his troops 'the soldiers immediately saluted him in the Macedonian tongue, and took up their shields, and striking them with their *sarissai*, raised the war-cry, summoning their enemies, since their leader was now at hand' (Plutarch, *Eumenes* 14.11). The charge was usually preceded by the discharge of missiles by the skirmishers, who then withdrew from the front lines:

> When the armies were within missile range, the Persians launched at Alexander such a shower of missiles that they collided with one another in the air, so thickly did they fly, and weakened the force of their impact. On both sides the trumpeters blew the signal of attack and then the Macedonians first raised an unearthly shout followed by the Persians answering, so that the whole hillside bordering the battlefield echoed back the sound. (Diodorus of Sicily, 17.33.3–4)

The passions aroused at such a time could, however, be detrimental to performance and, at Issus, Alexander was cautious to maintain formation and avoid tiring the infantry before they came to grips with the enemy.

Our knowledge of the actual fighting in the infantry sphere is, once again, limited by the nature of our sources. The Alexander historians tended, naturally, to focus on Alexander – in fact, the primary (some would say 'official') historian, Callisthenes of Olynthus, entitled his work

Praxeis Alexandrou ('The Deeds of Alexander') – and thus on the cavalry engagements. Hence the essential contributions of the phalanx are all but ignored. Furthermore, all our surviving sources, whether written in Greek or Latin, exhibit Roman coloring, and we are treated to contests with javelin and sword, with little information about the jousting of the *sarissophoroi*. For example the Sicilian Greek, Diodorus, dismisses the contribution of the infantry at Issus, after a lengthy description of the cavalry battle, in the following words:

> The Macedonian phalanx and the Persian infantry were engaged only briefly, for the rout of the [Persian] cavalry had been, as it were, a prelude of the whole victory. (17.34.9)

That there was more to the fighting at Issus we know from Arrian, who tells us that a gap in the center of the phalanx resulted in some desperate fighting and the deaths of phalangites and the taxiarch, Ptolemy son of Seleucus. But even Arrian gives no description of the actual infantry fighting. Quintus Curtius Rufus does provide details, but his is an imaginary scene intended to delight a Roman audience:

> The troops sent forward into the midst of the Persians were now totally surrounded and were stoutly defending themselves. But, being densely packed and virtually locked together, *they could not effectively hurl their javelins*, which, simultaneously discharged, became entangled with one another as they converged on the same targets … Thus, obliged to fight hand-to-hand, *they swiftly drew their swords*. Then the blood really flowed, for the two lines were so closely interlocked that they were striking each other's weapons with their own and driving their blades into their opponents' faces. It was now impossible for the timid or cowardly to remain inactive. Foot against foot, they were virtually fighting in single combat, standing in the same spot until they could make further room for themselves by winning their fight … The wounded could not retire from the battle as on other occasions because the enemy were bearing down on them in front while their own men were pushing them from behind. (3.11.4–6, emphasis added)

All this makes for sparkling journalism but, except for the reference to densely packed formations, it is not an accurate description of phalanx warfare. What makes the account even less credible is that Curtius Rufus later adds that in the entire battle only 32 infantrymen were killed, although 504 were wounded (3.11.27). Students of the Roman Republic will recognize similar descriptions in Livy's account of the Second Punic War (e.g. Livy, 23.27). What we can say with confidence is that a gap in the phalanx, as mentioned by Arrian, would have allowed the Greek mercenaries to take some of the *pezhetairoi* in the flank, where they wreaked havoc until the news of Darius' flight turned the tide of battle.

The pursuit of the enemy must have been left primarily to the cavalry and more lightly armed infantry, perhaps even the hypaspists, for it is hard to imagine that once the vanquished had put some distance between himself and the *pezhetairos* there was much hope of the *sarissa*-bearer running him down. Some may have dropped their *sarissai* and used their swords to finish off the wounded or those who had stumbled. It is reasonable to suppose that all troops participated in the despoiling of the dead and the looting of the enemy camp.

BELIEF AND BELONGING

Motives

It is by now a well-established belief that what makes a man fight is the bond that he feels with his comrades-in-arms: the men who are his family on the campaign, his emotional support, his 'confessors,' and his protectors in the line of battle. He fights with them and for them, and as much as he fears to let them down, he dreads even more the prospect and the stigma of dishonor. But what makes a man wage war is a more complex matter, the result of cultural conditioning and propaganda, of beliefs handed down from generation to generation and revelations of 'truths' (many of them fabricated to serve the occasion) that stir even the most indolent to follow the path of the war-god.

For the Macedonian phalangites, whose service under Alexander would take them to the ends of the known world and separate them from homeland and relatives for a decade or more, if not forever, the motives were manifold, ranging from simple greed and economics to the most lofty idealism. This warrior fought first and foremost because he was expected to, and it never occurred to him to challenge the demands of king and country, or even to question the basic premise that war is an inescapable fact of life. Indeed, he welcomed it as an opportunity to enter the arena of heroes, to test his mettle against the adversary, and to acquire the honor that ennobles all men, no matter how humble their origins. He was, in all likelihood, not highly educated, but he knew by heart the sagas of old, and the remarkable achievements of the Ten Thousand – the mercenaries who accompanied the Persian prince Cyrus to Cunaxa (near Babylon) and fought their way back along the valley of the Tigris, through the mountains of Armenia, and eventually to the Greek cities on the Black Sea. But he fought also for economic reasons, in the expectation of plunder, particularly in a campaign against the opulent barbarian. He fought out of reverence for his king, the defining characteristic of his people, and in this case for a king whose name was the byword for victory and daring:

> The Macedonians have a natural tendency to venerate their royalty, but even taking that into account, the extent of their admiration, or their burning affection, for this particular king [Alexander] is difficult to describe. First of all, they thought his every enterprise had divine aid. Fortune was with him at every turn and so even his rashness had produced glorious results …
> Then there are the things generally regarded as rather unimportant but which tend to find greater approval among soldiers: the fact that he exercised with his men, that he made his appearance and dress little different from an ordinary citizen's, that he had the energy of a soldier. (Curtius Rufus, 3.6.18–19)

Mercenaries and allies

Others who served Alexander fought as mercenaries, for pay, or as allied members of the League of Corinth, motivated by a desire to avenge the Persian 'atrocities' against Greece during the Persian Wars (490 and 480/79 BC). If the latter resounded with Macedonian infantrymen, it proved a double-edged sword, for when the allied troops were discharged after the capture of the Persian capitals – Babylon, Susa, Persepolis, and Ecbatana – or the death of Darius III, the Macedonians were expected to fight on. If they were satisfied with the prospect of world domination, they were soon disillusioned by the appointment of prominent barbarians to administrative posts and affronted by the king's attempts to integrate foreigners into Macedonian units. The phalangites were simple men, hardened by a life that promised them little more than self-sufficiency, and bound to their *taxeis* by kinship or shared geographical background. Their commanders were members of the local aristocracies, and they served them just as their own fathers had served theirs. Hence they were proud to declare their regional origins, as Lyncestians, Orestians, Elimiotes, or Tymphaeans. Reinforcements would have infiltrated their ranks on the same regional basis, bringing stories or even personal messages from home. Whether their units wore any outward signs of their shared backgrounds we do not know, but the pride and comfort that came from their common experience were evinced in the performance of the group and their rejection of change. Amongst themselves they spoke the Macedonian language, and probably even a local dialect of it. It is doubtful that many of them had a good understanding of Greek. It is highly likely that they prided themselves on being distinct even from the Macedonians of the plain, just as American southerners regarded Yankees with distrust if not loathing. Some *taxeis* of *pezhetairoi* were recruited from Lower Macedonia, but the evidence suggests that they were left at home with the regent Antipater, and the known taxiarchs are either identified as of Upper Macedonian origin or have names that suggest links with the highland aristocracy.

The elite hypaspist

For the hypaspists it was a different story. Like any elite force, they took pride in their special status as the king's guard. Membership was based on physical qualities as well as merit, but the demands were greater and life expectancy shorter. But their identity as a unit was unmistakable. Their equipment set them apart from the regular phalangites, and they were called upon more often and for the most arduous and dangerous tasks. They were the first on the city walls or the first through the breach, and their commanders had one of the highest mortality rates amongst the Macedonian officer class. Their sense of belonging was based on having 'walked the walk,' both as a unit and as individuals.

[At Troy, Alexander] made a gift of his armor to the temple [of Athena], and took in exchange, from where they were hung on the temple walls, some weapons which were still preserved from the Trojan war. These were supposed to have been carried before him by his hypaspists when he went into battle. (Arrian, 1.11.7–8)

The shield was what distinguished the hypaspists, and during the Indian campaign they decorated these with silver and took the name *argyraspids* ('silver shields'). The only thing they guarded more zealously than their king was their reputation. In the wars of Alexander's successors they surrendered another leader, Eumenes, to Antigonus and earned a reputation for perfidy, particularly in the historical account of Eumenes' kinsman, Hieronymus of Cardia. The later Hellenistic period witnessed units called *chrysaspides* ('golden shields'), *chalkaspides* ('bronze shields'), and *leukaspides* ('white shields') but they were neither direct descendants of Alexander's vaunted hypaspists nor their equals in battle.

Pederasty

It remains to consider one rather complex aspect of the soldier's sense of 'belonging:' the individual bond between comrades that involved 'sexual' relations or 'love.' Pederasty, the relationship between an older *erastes* and a younger *eromenos* (the object of the older man's affection), must be understood within the cultural context of ancient Greece and, in modern usage, the word 'pederasty' has connotations that the ancients would have found incomprehensible. We do know that such relationships were not only normal in Graeco-Macedonian military societies but also actually encouraged. In the case of the Macedonian warrior we do not have the kind of explicit evidence for institutionalized pederasty that exists for the Spartan or the Theban Sacred Band (who are specifically identified as 150 pairs of 'lovers'). We do know of intimate relationships between older men and younger 'boys' (and also about pairs of 'lovers' amongst the *hetairoi* and the pages) in Alexander'

The Lion of Chaeronea. Erected after the battle of Chaeronea (338 BC) as a monument to the Theban dead, the most famous of whom were the Sacred Band, destroyed by the forces led by Alexander (then only 18 years old) on the Macedonian left. The Sacred Band, perhaps the most famous individual unit in Greek history, comprised 150 pairs of homosexual lovers and ceased to exist after the Chaeronea disaster. (Author's collection)

army. And, although the best-known examples (Dimnus and Nicomachus; Hermolaus and Sostratus) are on record as plotting against Alexander, the same feelings that bound them to risk all in a conspiracy motivated them to give their lives for one another on the field of battle. That the ancients made a clear distinction between such relationships and effeminacy can be seen in the following episode:

> Pausanias was a Macedonian by birth who came from the area known as Orestis. He was a bodyguard [*somatophylax* = a member of royal hypaspists] of the King and because of his good looks had become Philip's lover. When Pausanias saw another Pausanias [the man happened to have the same name] receiving Philip's amorous attentions, he used insulting language to him, saying that he was effeminate and ready to submit to sex with anyone who wanted him. The fellow could not stand such malicious abuse … A few days later, when Philip was in combat with King Pleurias of Illyria, this second Pausanias stood before the King and on his own body took all the blows aimed at the King and thus died. (Diodorus of Sicily, 16.93.3–6)

EPILOGUE: DEFEAT OF THE INVINCIBLE PHALANX

Tradition held that Alexander received a response from the Pythian Oracle (Delphi) that he was 'invincible' (*aniketos*), and it was the practice of his troops as well, especially the later argyraspids (silver shields), to boast a record of unbroken victories dating back to their service under Philip.

> After Alexander the argyraspids had little respect for any leader [and] thought it an indignity to serve under others. Eumenes, therefore, proceeded with flattering entreaties … hailing them as 'comrades' and 'protectors,' now styling them variously his 'partners in the dangers of the East' and 'the last hope for his survival and his sole protection' … It was because of them that Alexander had become great, because of them that he had gained divine honors and deathless glory. (Justin, 14.6.7–10)

In truth, the phalanx had suffered a setback in the time of Philip, around 353, when the Phocians had employed artillery to great effect in the year before the famous battle of the Crocus Field. But the phalanx proved irresistible, even against the Romans in the time of Alexander's cousin, King Pyrrhus of Epirus, who suffered more from small numbers

The Lion of Amphipolis. Artistically less appealing than the Lion of Chaeronea, this is also a monument to the war-dead, but it was probably erected for cavalrymen rather than infantry. Statues to commemorate the dead at Granicus were made for members of the companion cavalry only. Status remained a factor, even in death (cf. Plutarch, *Eumenes* 9.5). Plutarch (*Alexander* 16.16) mistakenly implies that the statues made by Lysippus included the nine *pezhetairoi*, but this is either careless wording or an error on the biographer's part. (Archaeological Museum of Amfipoli) and attrition than tactical deficiency or lack of courage. But the reformed Roman army, with its more flexible maniples, proved too much for the Macedonian phalanx in the century and a half after Alexander's death. The ability of smaller units of Roman soldiers, protected by their larger shields, destroyed the integrity of the phalanx, especially when it fought on uneven ground.

> The most manifest cause of the Roman victory was the fact that there were many scattered engagements which first threw the wavering phalanx into disorder and then disrupted it completely. The strength of the phalanx is irresistible when it is close-packed and bristling with extended spears; but if by attacks at different points you force the troops to swing round their spears, unwieldy as they are by reason of their length and weight, they become entangled in a disorderly mass; and further, the noise of any commotion on the flank or in the rear throws them into confusion, and then the whole formation collapses. This is what happened in this battle [the battle of Pydna, 168], when the phalanx was forced to meet the Romans who were attacking in small groups, with the Macedonian line broken at many points. The Romans kept infiltrating their files at every place where a gap offered. If they had made a frontal attack with their whole line against an orderly phalanx, the Romans would have impaled themselves on the spears and would not have withstood the dense formation. (Livy, 44.41)

'Macedonian' troops, that is, infantrymen equipped like *pezhetairoi*, fought at Magnesia against Roman forces, but the result was the same. The glory days of the phalanx had passed. But the second half of the fourth century belonged to Macedonian arms, especially the *sarissa*. Perhaps the best way of concluding an account of the Macedonian infantry warrior is by quoting the words of Quintus Curtius Rufus, commenting on the Macedonian victory at Gaugamela:

> If we want a fair assessment of the Macedonians of the day, we shall have to say that the King truly deserved such subjects and his subjects such a king. (4.16.33)

MUSEUMS AND WEBSITES

Artifacts relating to Graeco-Macedonian warfare can be found in major museums around the world, including of course London's British Museum. Two of the most spectacular battle scenes from antiquity relating to Alexander the Great are the Alexander Sarcophagus, on display in the Istanbul Archaeological Museum, and the Alexander Mosaic in the Museo Archeologico Nazionale in Naples. Remains from the so-called 'Tomb of Philip II' can be viewed at the Archaeological Museum in Thessaloniki, Greece. Smaller museums in Dion, Pella, and Amfipoli (Amphipolis) are worth a visit. For the military enthusiast, the National Museum in Athens and the museum at the archaeological site of Olympia, which has an impressive collection of weapons and armor, are a must.

The two most comprehensive websites on Alexander are http://www.isidore-of-seville.com/Alexanderama.html, maintained by Timothy Spalding, and the very lively http://www.pothos.org/, both of which have links to other important websites.

See also Sander van Dorst's site on the Macedonian army: http://members.tripod.com/~S_van_Dorst/Alexander.html.

Lastly, for a comprehensive and regularly updated bibliography of Alexander Studies, consult http://hum.ucalgary.ca/wheckel/alexande.htm.

Damaged figure of a Persian infantryman from the Alexander Sarcophagus of Sidon. Unfortunately his weapons are lost, but his outfit appears in no way different from that of the cavalryman at his back. (Archaeological Museum, Istanbul)

GLOSSARY

agema A guard unit, that is, a special unit of the hypaspists. The size of the unit and the criteria for selection are unknown. It is tempting to see them as a force of 300, with 100 men drawn from each of the three chiliarchies, but this cannot be proved. They may be identical to the royal hypaspists.

antilabe The handgrip of the shield. This is attested for the hoplite shield; although there is no evidence for it, the smaller *pelte* of the phalangite must have been equipped with one for use in emergencies.

archihypaspistes Commander to the 3,000 regular hypaspists.

argyraspids 'Silver shields:' elite unit of 3,000. Formerly the hypaspists of Alexander. They were at least partially disbanded in 317/16 BC.

asthetairoi In most cases referred to as 'the so-called *asthetairoi*.' A group, perhaps three or four *taxeis*, of *pezhetairoi*. What distinguished them from the remainder of the *pezhetairoi* is not entirely certain.

chiliarch Commander of a thousand (i.e. 1,024 men).

cubit From the word for elbow (*cubitum*), a measurement derived from the distance between the elbow and the fingers (roughly 18in).

dekas Plural *dekades*. Originally, as the name implies, a unit of ten men. This was expanded to 16. Sixteen *dekades* formed a *lochos*. See also *syntagma*.

dimoirites An NCO who received double pay. Under the system envisioned by Alexander in 323, each *dekas* would include, in addition to its leader, the dekadarch, one *dimoirites* and two 'ten-stater' men, who earned less than the *dimoirites*.

drachma There were 6,000 drachmae in a talent. Six obols (*oboloi* or *obeloi*) made up a drachma. One drachma per day represented a respectable day's wage for an infantryman or a rower in the fleet.

hamippoi Literally, those who were 'with the horses:' infantrymen who fought on foot among the cavalry. Sometimes they held on to the horses' tails in order to keep contact. One of their tasks was to dispatch those of the enemy who had been unhorsed by the Macedonian cavalrymen.

hemithorakion The 'half breastplate,' which offered protection only to the front of the body.

hetairoi The companions of the king, both the high-ranking military-political advisors and the aristocratic cavalry.

hoplon The heavy, concave shield of the hoplite. About 3ft in diameter. Although the plural *hopla* could mean 'shields' it was often used in a general sense to mean 'arms.'

hypaspistai Singular *hypaspistes*. Hypaspists ('shield bearers'), apparently 3,000 in number (that is, three chiliarchies).

hypaspistai basilikoi Royal hypaspists. Troops of aristocratic descent, they formed the pool from which future officers were drawn.

knemis Plural *knemides*. Greaves.

lochos Plural *lochoi*. In Alexander's time, a unit of c.250 men (16 *dekades* = 1 *lochos*: 16 x 16 = 256). Four *lochoi* made up a chiliarchy; six constituted a *taxis*.

othismos The infantry 'push.'

paides basilikoi The 'royal pages.' These were sons (13 to 18 years old) of prominent Macedonians raised at the court. They accompanied the king on the hunt, and sometimes into battle (though normally in less dangerous positions). They later became *hypaspistai basilikoi* or officers of one sort or another.

palm Ancient measurement. Four palms were roughly equivalent to a foot. The shield of the phalangite was said to be eight palms in diameter.

pelte The lighter shield of the targeteers, peltasts. A version of this was adopted by the Macedonian phalangites. About 2ft in diameter.

pentakosiarch Commander of 500 (i.e. 512 men).

pezhetairoi Literally 'foot companions' or 'infantry companions.' The name was originally used of Philip's elite guards, but these were renamed *hypaspistai* by Alexander and the name *pezhetairoi* was given to the regionally recruited heavy infantry.

porpax The 'sleeve' in the center of the *hoplon* or *aspis*, through which the arm was passed in order to grip the *antilabe*.

sarissa (Also *sarisa*.) The Macedonian pike. In Alexander's time, it reached a maximum of 18ft in length.

stade (Greek: *stadion*.) This was a measurement of 600ft, but the exact length of the 'foot' varied. Hence ten stades would be in the range of 1.14 miles.

synaspismos The locking together of shields, in close formation; normally for defensive purposes.

syntagma Plural *syntagmata*. The later name for the *lochos* of Alexander's time.

taxis Plural *taxeis*. The most important unit (the battalion or brigade) of the *pezhetairoi*, comprising six *lochoi* for a total of roughly 1,500 men.

BIBLIOGRAPHY

Ancient sources

Aeneas Tacticus, Asclepiodotus, Onasander, translated by the Illinois Greek Club, Loeb Classical Library no. 156 (Cambridge, Mass., 1923)

Arrian, *The Campaigns of Alexander*, translated by A. de Sélincourt, with notes by J. R. Hamilton, Penguin Classics (London, 1971)

Austin, M. M., *The Hellenistic World from Alexander to the Roman Conquest: A Selection of Ancient Sources in Translation* (Cambridge, 1981)

Diodorus of Sicily, translated and edited by C. Bradford Welles, Loeb Classical Library, vol. VIII (Cambridge, Mass., 1963)

Frontinus, translated by Charles E. Bennett, Loeb Classical Library (Cambridge, Mass., 1925)

Justin, *Epitome of the Philippic History of Pompeius Trogus*, books 11–12: *Alexander the Great*, translated by J. C. Yardley, with commentary by Waldemar Heckel, Clarendon Ancient History Series (Oxford, 1997)

Livy, *The Dawn of the Roman Empire*, translated by J. C. Yardley, Oxford World's Classics (Oxford 2000)

Plutarch, *The Age of Alexander*, translated by Ian Scott-Kilvert, Penguin Classics (London, 1973)

Polyaenus, *Stratagems of War*, edited and translated by Peter Krentz and Everett L. Wheeler. 2 vols, Ares Press (Chicago, 1994)

Polybius, *The Histories*, translated by W. R. Paton. 6 vols. Loeb Classical Library (Cambridge, Mass., 1922–1927)

Quintus Curtius Rufus, *The History of Alexander*, translated by J. C. Yardley, with introduction and notes by Waldemar Heckel, Penguin Classics (London, 1984)

Modern works

F. E. Adcock, *The Greek and Macedonian Art of War*, University of California Press (Berkeley and Los Angeles, 1957)

J. K. Anderson, 'Hoplite Weapons and Offensive Arms,' in Hanson (ed.), *Hoplites: The Classical Greek Battle Experience*, 15–37, Routledge, an imprint of Taylor & Francis Books Ltd (London, 1991)

A. B. Bosworth, *Conquest and Empire. The Reign of Alexander the Great*, Cambridge University Press (Cambridge, 1988)

A. B. Bosworth, *Alexander and the East. The Tragedy of Triumph*, Oxford University Press (Oxford, 1996)

Peter Connolly, *The Greek Armies*, Greenhill Books (London, 1977)

Albert M. Devine, 'Alexander the Great,' in Sir John Hackett (ed.), *Warfare in the Ancient World*, 104–29, Checkmark Books (London, 1989)

Theodore Ayrault Dodge, *Alexander. A History of the Origin and Growth of the Art of War from the Earliest Times to the Battle of Ipsus, 301 BC, with a detailed account of the great Macedonian* (Boston, 1890, reprinted Da Capo Press, 1996). Still useful.

D. W. Engels, *Alexander the Great and the Logistics of the Macedonian Army*, University of California Press (Berkeley and Los Angeles, 1978)

Paul Faure, *La vie quotidienne des armées d'Alexandre*, Hachette (Paris, 1982)

Arther Ferrill, *The Origins of War from the Stone Age to Alexander the Great*, Thames and Hudson Ltd (London, 1985)

J. F. C. Fuller, *The Generalship of Alexander the Great*, Da Capo Press (New Brunswick, NJ, 1960)

G. T. Griffith and N. G. L. Hammond, *A History of Macedonia*, vol. 2, Oxford University Press (Oxford, 1979)

Debra Hamel, *Athenian Generals. Military Authority in the Classical Period*, Brill (Leiden, 1998)

J. R. Hamilton, *Alexander the Great*, University of Pittsburgh Press (Pittsburgh, 1974)

N. G. L. Hammond, *Alexander the Great. King, Commander and Statesman*, Chatto and Windus (London, 1981)

N. G. L. Hammond, *The Macedonian State. The Origins, Institutions and History*, Oxford University Press (Oxford, 1989)

N. G. L. Hammond, *The Genius of Alexander the Great*, University of North Carolina Press (Chapel Hill, 1997)

N. G. L. Hammond and F. W. Walbank, *A History of Macedonia*, vol. 3, Oxford University Press (Oxford, 1988)

Victor Davis Hanson (ed.), *Hoplites: The Classical Greek Battle Experience*, Routledge, an imprint of Taylor & Francis Books Ltd (London, 1991)

Victor Davis Hanson, 'Hoplite Technology in Phalanx Battle,' in Hanson (ed.), *Hoplites*: 63–84

Waldemar Heckel, *The Marshals of Alexander's Empire*, Routledge, an imprint of Taylor & Francis Books Ltd (London, 1992)

Waldemar Heckel, *The Wars of Alexander the Great, 336–323 BC*, Osprey, Essential Histories no. 26 (Oxford, 2002)

Frank L. Holt, *Into the Land of Bones. Alexander the Great in Afghanistan*, University of California Press (Berkeley and Los Angeles, 2005)

Paul Bentley Kern, *Ancient Siege Warfare*, Souvenir Press Ltd (Bloomington, 1999)

J. E. Lendon, *Soldiers and Ghosts. A History of Battle in Classical Antiquity*, Yale University Press (New Haven, 2005)

Minor Markle III, 'The Macedonian Sarissa, Spear, and Related Armor,' *American Journal of Archaeology* 81, 323–39 (1977)

E. W. Marsden, *The Campaign of Gaugamela*, Liverpool University Press (Liverpool, 1964)

R. D. Milns, 'The Hypaspists of Alexander III,' *Historia* 20, 186–95 (1971)

R. D. Milns, 'Army Pay and the Military Budget of Alexander the Great,' in W. Will (ed.), *Zu Alexander dem Grossen*, Festschrift G. Wirth, 2 vols, 1.233–56 (Amsterdam, 1987)

W. K. Pritchett, *The Greek State at War*, Part III, University of California Press (Berkeley and Los Angeles, 1979)

Michael M. Sage, *Warfare in Ancient Greece. A Sourcebook*, Routledge, an imprint of Taylor & Francis Books Ltd (London, 1996)

Nick Sekunda and John Warry, *Alexander the Great: His Armies and Campaigns 334–323 BC*, Osprey (Oxford, 1998)

A. M. Snodgrass, *Arms and Armor of the Greeks*, Thames and Hudson Ltd (London 1967; revised ed. Baltimore, 1999)

John Warry, *Alexander 334–323 BC: Conquest of the Persian Empire*. Osprey, Campaign no. 7 (Oxford, 1991)

COLOR PLATE COMMENTARY

A: THE PHALANGITE (*PEZHETAIROS*)

A close view of the Macedonian phalangite in full armor. The soldier wears the Phrygian helmet, with cheek pieces, which allows better hearing and visibility than the old Corinthian-style helmets of the Greek hoplites of the Archaic and Classical periods. The soldier is bearded, despite the commonly accepted view that Alexander required his troops to shave their beards in the belief that facial hair gave the enemy something to clutch in close combat (Polyaenus, *Strat.* 4.3.2). If this story is true – and there are certainly clean-shaven warriors on the Alexander Sarcophagus – it need not have applied to the phalangites, for whom close, individual combat was undesirable.

The warrior is protected by a *linothorax*, worn over the short-sleeved *exomis*, the bottom of which extends beyond the corselet itself. The various layers of linen that made up the corselet are illustrated at the upper right, and these show coarser linen on the inside and smoother layers on the outside. The weight of the corselet is about 11–14lb, and thus considerably lighter than the leather, bronze, and (especially) iron cuirasses that were worn by some infantry and cavalrymen. The skirt of the corselet, made up of 'wings' (*pteruges*), is loose and unstiffened for ease of movement.

A leather baldric slung over the shoulder supports the smaller shield – about 2ft in diameter and less concave than the larger *hoplon*. Details of the outside of the shield, with the embossed eight-rayed star of the Macedonian kingdom, can be seen at the bottom left. In battle, the soldier's forearm would have been drawn through the *porpax* in the inside center, but the hand would have been free to grasp the 18ft *sarissa*, which because of its length and weight required the

Iron cuirass from the Tomb of Philip II in Vergina. It had gold decoration and would have had leather *pteruges* attached to the bottom. (Archaeological Museum, Thessaloniki)

LEFT **Lion hunt scene on a mosaic from the House of Dionysus in Pella. It is thought by some to depict the figures of Alexander and Craterus (presumably the figure on the left, wearing the *kausia*). The figure on the right is about to strike with a *kopis*. The sheath of the sword, shown in each man's left hand, would have been made of wood and bone. (Archaeological Museum of Pella, Ann Ronan Picture Library)**

use of both hands. Nevertheless, the illustration shows a handgrip (*antilabe*), without which the shield would have been all but useless to a phalangite out of formation.

The end of the *sarissa* – the full extent and the size of the *sarissa* in relation to its bearer are shown in the miniature to the bottom right – bears a butt spike like the one found at the ancestral Macedonian capital of Aegae (Vergina), and it becomes clear that it constituted almost two-thirds of that part of the *sarissa* that extended behind the phalangite when it was leveled in drill or combat. Both the *sarissa* head and the butt spike are shown in detail on the right side of the page. Here one sees also the coupling link or collar, of which only one example has been found to date, though it is clear that all *sarissai* must have had them. This coupling link joined the two parts of the sarissa and allowed it to be dismantled on the march (as shown in the top left-hand corner); it also made repair quicker and less expensive, and allowed replacement parts to be more easily transported. The illustration of the *sarissa* in two halves is based on Mr Ryan Jones' own experiments with a *sarissa* reconstructed according to the weights and measurements of the archaeological finds.

Finally, the warrior has slung at his side a *kopis*. The name of this slashing sword means 'chopper' or 'cleaver,' and although ancient terminology is inconsistent, it is clear from Xenophon's time that the term *kopis* was used interchangeably with *machaira*. It is the *machaira* that is mentioned as part of the infantryman's equipment in the

Amphipolis regulations from the time of Philip V. The illustration shows the curved handle, which gave some protection to the knuckles and allowed for a more secure grip. It should be noted that Plate A shows the phalangite par excellence, and a man thus equipped would have fought in the front ranks. Towards the center and the rear there would have been many infantrymen who lacked the *linothorax* or who wore the less protective (although, admittedly, more comfortable) slouch-hat known as the *kausia*.

B: *PEZHETAIROI* IN TRAINING

In their elementary training in the use of the *sarissa* in formation, the *pezhetairoi* wore only the *exomis*, as pictured here. But many drills and conditioning exercises required the soldiers to march with full equipment and rations. In practice, the butt spike of the *sarissa* was almost as potent a weapon as the *sarissa* head, and since the *sarissa* was held at a point that allowed 12–15ft to project in front, with 3ft extending to the rear, it was essential that the soldier learn to position himself in relation to his comrades in the formation in such a way as to provide maximum danger to the enemy and protection against the *sarissa*-ends of his own colleagues.

The first five of the 16 rows of the *syntagma* were so closely packed together that, when their *sarissai* were leveled, even that of the fifth man projected in front of the file leader. To allow for such a dense formation, each man must have been stationed behind the next, with the extended *sarissa* gripped at nearly the same point where he was level with the butt spike of the man in front of him. Exit from the file, in the event of injury or loss of weapons, could thus only

BELOW **Three-barbed arrowhead with PHILIPPOU ('of Philip' or 'belonging to Philip'). This was the head of a catapult dart found at Olynthus and dates perhaps from the time of the city's siege in 348 BC. (Archaeological Museum, Thessaloniki)**

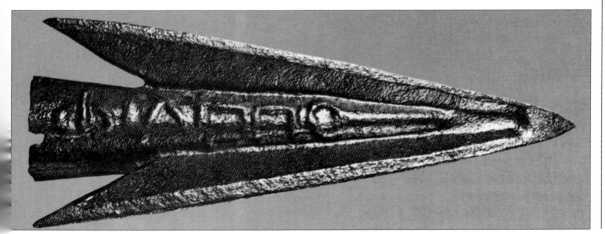

have been possible by moving to the left and backwards through whatever alley the formation allowed. Those in rows six and higher elevated their *sarissai* in stages until those standing from about the middle to the back held their weapons upright.

This arrangement was also advantageous in that it protected the phalangites from projectiles launched by the enemy's archers, slingers, and javelin-men. Furthermore, the gradual elevation of the *sarissai* towards the middle involved a concomitant raising of the shields for added protection.

The basic formation, which here (for the sake of convenience) is referred to as a *syntagma*, represented 256 men, 16 deep and 16 abreast. The arrangement is shown schematically at the bottom left. To the bottom right we see the alignment of *sarissa*-bearers in a single file. Six *syntagmata*, to use the terminology of the later tacticians (though in Alexander's time they may have been called *lochoi*), made up a *taxis*. For most of Alexander's Asiatic campaign there were six such *taxeis* deployed in the Macedonian center.

C: EQUIPMENT

(1) Phrygian-style helmet, with plumes inserted in the holders located on the left and right sides, as well as a plume on the crest.

(2) Thracian helmet with cheek pieces and a narrow crest. This crest could have been attached by means of rivets, as

Wallpainting from Lefkadia (c.250 BC). Thracian helmet with crest and cheek pieces (very similar to the one illustrated on page 13). (Ekdotike Athenon SA, Athens)

Detail from the Boscoreale Mural, showing Antigonus Gonatas wearing the *kausia* and diadem. Some have argued that the individual pictured is female, and others that it is Alexander's son by Rhoxane. (Ekdotike Athenon SA, Athens)

a surviving example of a Thracian helmet, missing the crest, suggests.

(3) The 'Vergina' helmet. This is similar to the Phrygian helmet, but whereas the Phrygian helmet tapers gradually towards a more rounded (lobate) crest, the crest in this case sits virtually straight and narrow atop the helmet. Made of iron, the 'Vergina' helmet is an extraordinary find and was certainly not used by the common phalangite.

(4) A bronze thorax, hinged on one side. The wearer entered the armor from the side. The hinges were equipped with removable pins, to allow the breastplate to be opened completely; they would be replaced once the armor was fitted around the warrior. Beside the hinges can be seen loops through which small leather laces were passed to help secure the breastplate, in case a pin fell out. The warrior was thus locked into a breastplate that weighed as much as 25–30lb.

(5) Bronze *hemithorakion*, or 'half-thorax,' which gave protection to only the front of the body. Alexander is said to have employed this armor as means of discouraging his troops from turning their backs to the enemy.

(6) Iron cuirass. This unique piece of armor was made to look like the *linothorax*, the common armor of the period, but was fashioned out of iron plates covered with leather and adorned with gold. Fashion and status continued to be factors for the military and political elite.

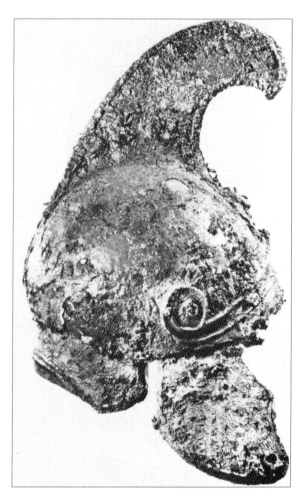

The Vergina Helmet, made of iron. (Archaeological Museum, Thessaloniki)

(7) Two swords. The straighter and shorter *xiphos* – both edges were used for cutting, and it served also as a thrusting weapon – and the *kopis* ('cleaver'), the curved slashing sword, with a protective handle.

8. *Linothorax*, with two rows of flexible 'wings' (*pteruges*) for better maneuvering. The *linothorax* could weigh 11–14lb, which made it a far more attractive choice for the wearer than the 30lb bronze cuirass. Some examples in contemporary art seem to indicate that the small plates in the form of scales or various other decorations would be riveted onto the *linothorax* to provide increased protection without much additional weight. The multiple layers of linen worked to slow the spear or swordthrust as it passed through each layer; the design is similar to modern Kevlar vests.

D: THE PHALANX MEETS MILITARY TECHNOLOGY

At Gaugamela (331 BC), Darius III attempted to disrupt the Macedonian phalanx by driving scythe-bearing chariots into their ranks. This tactic was countered by the phalanx in a number of ways, as instructed by Alexander. The ancient sources speak for themselves:

Against the threat of the scythed chariots, he ordered the infantry of the phalanx to join shields as soon as these went into action against them and to beat the shields with their sarissai, creating such a din as to frighten the horses into bolting to the rear, or, if they persevered, to open gaps in the ranks such that they might ride through harmlessly. (Diodorus of Sicily, 17.57.6)

Arrian's account says:

The Persians sent their scythe-chariots into action … in the hope of throwing Alexander's line into confusion. But in this they were disappointed; for the chariots were no sooner off the mark than they were met by the missile weapons of the Agrianes and Balacrus' javelin-throwers [akontistai], who were stationed in advance of the companion cavalry; again, they seized the reins and dragged the drivers to the ground, then surrounded the horses and cut them down. Some few of the vehicles succeeded in passing through, but to no purpose, for the Macedonians [i.e. the infantry] had orders, wherever they attacked, to break formation and let them through deliberately. (3.13.5–6)

Arrian goes on to say that the chariots and drivers drove through the alleys created by the phalanx and were finished off by the troops stationed at the rear. He also implies that there was no significant harm done to the Macedonians. Diodorus, however, shows that this was not the case:

In some instances the horse were killed by javelin casts and in others they rode through and escaped, but some of them, using the full force of their momentum and applying their steel blades actively, wrought death among the Macedonians in many and various forms. Such was the keenness and the force of the scythes ingeniously contrived to do harm that they severed the arms of many, shields and all, and in no small number of cases they cut through necks and sent heads tumbling to the ground with eyes still open and the expression of the countenance unchanged, and in other cases they were sliced through the ribs with mortal gashes and inflicted a quick death. (17.58.4–5)

E: REALITY – THE WEAKNESS OF THE PHALANGITE IN HAND-TO-HAND FIGHTING

The strength of the Macedonian phalanx, just like that of the Greek hoplite phalanx, was its ability to present a solid unit, an impenetrable wall of shields and spears, to the enemy. But as an individual, the phalangite or *pezhetairos* was ineffective. The *sarissa* was too long for fighting at close range, and it easily upset the balance of the warrior himself when fighting out of formation. Furthermore, the small *pelte* offered only limited protection to the body. Quintus Curtius Rufus (9.7.16–26) and Diodorus of Sicily (quoted below) give very similar accounts of a duel between a Greek athlete, Dioxippus, armed only with a cloak and club, and a Macedonian phalangite in full armor named Corrhagus. These accounts, based on the same primary source – presumably Cleitarchus – suggest that the javelin was also part of the equipment of the *pezhetairos*. This is misleading, since the massed combat and *monomachia* (single-combat) presented two completely different situations.

There was a certain Macedonian called Corrhagus who had been accepted as one of the Companions. He was possessed of remarkable physical strength and had frequently performed courageous acts in battle. Under the influence of drink, Corrhagus challenged Dioxippus the Athenian, an athlete who had won the garland for the most prestigious victories in the games, to face him in single combat. The other guests at the party spurred on the men's rivalry, as one might expect; Dioxippus accepted the challenge and the King fixed a date for the match. When the time for the contest arrived, men assembled in their tens of thousands to watch. Being of the same race, the Macedonians and the King strongly supported Corrhagus, while the Greeks were behind Dioxippus. As the men came forward to the event the Macedonian was equipped with splendid weapons; the Athenian was naked and smeared with oil, and he carried an appropriately sized club.

The physical strength and superb prowess of the two men provoked general admiration, and it was as though what was expected to take place was a contest between gods. The Macedonian aroused sheer amazement for his physical condition and dazzling arms, and some resemblance to Ares was noticed in him. Dioxippus, on the other hand, had the look of Heracles, being the superior of the two in strength and also because of his athletic training – and still more because of the identifying characteristic of the club.

As they advanced on each other, the Macedonian, at an appropriate remove, hurled his javelin, but the other man swerved slightly and avoided the blow that was aimed at him. Then Corrhagus went forward with his Macedonian sarissa leveled before him but, as he approached, Dioxippus struck the sarissa with his club and broke it. Having thus encountered two setbacks, the Macedonian was now reduced to fighting with the sword; but just as he was about to draw the weapon Dioxippus moved first and jumped at him. As Corrhagus was drawing the blade, Dioxippus grabbed his sword-hand with his own left hand and with the other pulled his rival off balance and made him trip over. His antagonist thrown to earth, the Greek set his foot on the man's neck, held up his club, and turned his gaze to the spectators.

The crowd was in uproar over this unexpected turn of events and the display of extraordinary bravado. The King ordered the man's release, terminated the spectacle and left, furious at the Macedonian's defeat. Releasing his fallen antagonist, Dioxippus went off with a notable victory, and with a garland presented to him by his countrymen for having brought to the Greeks a glory that they all shared. (Diodorus, 17.100–101)

F: CAMPAIGNING: HYPASPISTS AND *PEZHETAIROI* ON BROKEN GROUND, THE THRACIAN CAMPAIGN OF 336/5 BC

Rugged terrain has always challenged the phalanx, but in his campaign against the so-called 'autonomous' Thracians, Alexander was able to maintain the cohesion of his forces in a mountain pass and to avoid the wagons of the Thracians that were being rolled down to disrupt his formations. By placing the less mobile *pezhetairoi* in the more level areas, where they could form alleys for the wagons to pass through, he kept the main portion of the phalanx intact and ready to meet the enemy if he should rush down the hill. The more difficult ground was occupied by the hypaspists, who were unencumbered by the *sarissa* and carried larger shields, which they placed over their bodies to allow the wagons to pass over without doing serious harm. Arrian describes the incident but makes no distinction between the two types of troops. But clearly it would have been impossible for the *pezhetairoi*, with smaller and less concave shields, to find protection under them, to say nothing of the difficulty of grounding the *sarissai* in massed formation.

Thracian helmet, very similar to that illustrated on the tomb painting (page 13). There appear to be traces on the top of holes for the attachment of a metal crest. (Staatliche Museen, Berlin)

Alexander sent orders to his hoplites that whenever the carts tumbled down the slope, those who were on level ground and could break formation were to part to right and left, leaving an avenue for the carts; those caught in the narrows were to crouch close together; and some were actually to fall to the ground and link their shields closely together so that when the carts came at them they were likely to bound over them by their gathered impetus and pass without doing harm. (Arrian, 1.1.8–9)

In this way the Thracians were unable to disrupt the Macedonian phalanx and come to grips with it while it was in disarray. The hypaspists, once the danger had passed, continued uphill on the left side, led by Alexander and protected by the covering fire of the archers. The Thracians were dislodged from their position with ease.

G: THE AFTERMATH OF BATTLE

Despite Alexander's much celebrated triumphs over Persia and over a king who had twice fled from the battlefield, victory in battle came at a cost, especially for the infantrymen, whose casualties were always (with the notable exception of the battle of the Granicus) far greater than those of the cavalry. The numbers of dead infantry are almost certainly deflated for purposes of propaganda, for it did not pay to have Alexander's official historian sending home realistic casualty figures. Hence we are told that about 300 infantrymen were killed at Issus, although the hard fighting against the 30,000 Greek mercenaries in the center (where the taxiarch Ptolemy son of Seleucus was killed) make this number risible. An anonymous historical papyrus found at Oxyrhynchus in Egypt gives a more reasonable figure of 1,000 infantry and 200 cavalry killed on the Macedonian side. We do not know, of course, how many of these were *pezhetairoi* or hypaspists, but we must remember also that many of the wounded either died afterwards or were invalided home (or left behind as garrison troops).

Plate G shows one of the most gruesome scenes that would have confronted the warrior: the recovery of the dead and wounded from the battlefield. Two men are shown carrying a man's corpse to be loaded on a wagon. Hours before, they had known him alive, perhaps discussing their chances in the coming struggle or standing shoulder to shoulder with him in the actual fighting. Others support and console a wounded comrade, while others still pick through the debris, salvaging usable weapons or despoiling the dead. The Persian dead are recognizable by their scaled armor and their peculiar shields. Of the two types illustrated here, the rectangular shield was used by Persian infantrymen in the fifth and fourth centuries, and the other appears frequently in Greek vase paintings and the Alexander Sarcophagus.

H: THE ELITE INFANTRYMAN, THE HYPASPIST

Two members of the hypaspist corps are illustrated, one wearing the Thracian helmet, the other one of the 'Vergina' type. What makes the hypaspists distinct from the *pezhetairoi* is the use of 'hoplite' equipment. The offensive weapon is the spear (*dory*), some 7–8ft in length, including spearhead and butt spike (the *sauroter* or 'lizard killer'). Defensively, the *hoplon*, the larger and more concave, rimmed shield, or *aspis*, is the feature from which the unit takes its name – *hypaspistai* or 'shield-bearers.' Normally, the distance from the *porpax* to the *antilabe* would have been a little less than a cubit, since the arm was drawn through the *porpax* up to the inside of the elbow joint and the *antilabe* was gripped in a closed hand. Hence the diameter of the shield tended to be roughly 3ft. Such shields are also depicted on Macedonian tomb paintings, though one must distinguish in some cases between ceremonial and functional shields.

The rest of the hypaspist's equipment differed little from that of a front-line *pezhetairos*. In this illustration the central figure wears the bronze thorax, with *pteruges* attached; the one to the right and in the distance wears the *linothorax*. Both wear the short-sleeved *exomis*, bronze greaves and sandals.

Wallpainting from Lefkadia. Tomb of Lyson and Callicles. Helmet with plumes and cheek pieces, of the type depicted in Plate H. The reddish-brown color on the inside of the cheek piece may indicate an attached leather pad. (Ekdotike Athenon SA, Athens)

INDEX

Figures in **bold** refer to illustrations